Walrus

T0345305

Animal

Series editor: Jonathan Burt

Already published

Albatross Graham Barwell · *Ant* Charlotte Sleigh · *Ape* John Sorenson · *Bear* Robert E. Bieder

Bee Claire Preston · *Camel* Robert Irwin · *Cat* Katharine M. Rogers · *Chicken* Annie Potts

Cockroach Marion Copeland · *Cow* Hannah Velten · *Crocodile* Dan Wylie

Crow Boria Sax · *Deer* John Fletcher · *Dog* Susan McHugh · *Dolphin* Alan Rauch

Donkey Jill Bough · *Duck* Victoria de Rijke · *Eel* Richard Schweid · *Elephant* Dan Wylie

Falcon Helen Macdonald *Fly* Steven Connor · *Fox* Martin Wallen · *Frog* Charlotte Sleigh

Giraffe Edgar Williams · *Gorilla* Ted Gott and Kathryn Weir · *Hare* Simon Carnell

Hedgehog Hugh Warwick · *Horse* Elaine Walker · *Hyena* Mikita Brottman

Kangaroo John Simons · *Leech* RobertG. W. Kirk and Neil Pemberton

Leopard Desmond Morris · *Lion* Deirdre Jackson · *Lobster* Richard J. King

Monkey Desmond Morris · *Moose* Kevin Jackson · *Mosquito* Richard Jones

Octopus Richard Schweid · *Ostrich* Edgar Williams · *Otter* Daniel Allen · *Owl* Desmond Morris

Oyster Rebecca Stott · *Parrot* Paul Carter · *Peacock* Christine E. Jackson · *Penguin* Stephen Martin

Pig Brett Mizelle · *Pigeon* Barbara Allen · *Rabbit* Victoria Dickenson · *Rat* Jonathan Burt

Rhinoceros Kelly Enright · *Salmon* Peter Coates · *Shark* Dean Crawford · *Snail* Peter Williams

Snake Drake Stutesman · *Sparrow* Kim Todd · *Spider* Katja and Sergiusz Michalski

Swan Peter Young · *Tiger* Susie Green · *Tortoise* Peter Young · *Trout* James Owen

Vulture Thom van Dooren · *Walrus* John Miller and Louise Miller · *Whale* Joe Roman

Wolf Garry Marvin

Walrus

John Miller and Louise Miller

REAKTION BOOKS

For Dave Miller (1944–2013): il miglior tricheco

Published by
REAKTION BOOKS LTD
33 Great Sutton Street
London EC1V 0DX, UK
www.reaktionbooks.co.uk

Printed and bound in China by 1010 Printing International Ltd

A catalogue record for this book is available from the British Library

ISBN 978 1 78023 291 1

Contents

1 The Walrus Emerges 7
2 Walruses and the Indigenous Arctic 42
3 The War on the Walrus 73
4 Walruses in Popular and Visual Culture 109
5 Walruses in a Warming World 147
   Timeline 172
   References 174
   Select Bibliography 186
   Associations and Websites 189
   Acknowledgements 192
   Photo Acknowledgements 193
   Index 195

1 The Walrus Emerges

'I am the walrus', claimed John Lennon in 1967, although no one is entirely sure what exactly he meant by that. To an extent the song's strangeness is lost now in its iconic status. It is easy to forget the oddity of the lyrics in this instantly recognizable classic. The walrus itself appears to us in a similar mixture of weirdness and familiarity. Its unique appearance makes it one of the most easily identified – and anthropomorphized – of animals. But the more you think about walruses, the stranger they seem. As one marine biologist put it, 'if walruses did not exist, inventing them might strain the imagination'.[1] Huge, lumbering and stinking, walruses exhibit a high level of social organization along with complex emotional lives and, perhaps more surprisingly, evidence of musicality and even creativity. Yet their behaviour and life cycle are still only partially understood. Scientists face significant obstacles in studying the walrus in its remote Arctic and sub-Arctic habitats. With global warming bringing radical changes to the geography of the North, time for further research into walruses in their natural environment may be limited.

Popular culture has made the walrus comical: whiskery, bleary-eyed and bellowing, a favourite uncle back from his regimental reunion ready for a nice long sleep in front of the fire; the genial fat man of the animal kingdom. The walrus is the Homer Simpson of the sea: slow, dense, fond of food and sleep, kindly and humorous.

An Atlantic walrus resting on the ice.

7

A male Pacific walrus covered in tubercles (warty lumps) emerges from the sea.

In nature documentaries walrus herds, known as haul-outs when out of water, form one of the defining images of the Arctic. Sometimes many thousands of animals may gather on an ice floe, dozing and grunting as they lie all over each other. For the most part walruses are peaceable, but they can be fierce when threatened. To early European sailors venturing into Arctic waters, these were terrifying monsters of the deep, intent on consigning the unwary to a watery grave. In fact, it was the walrus that had more cause for fear: its ivory tusks, oil-rich blubber and thick hide made it a prime target for commercial hunters. The malign sea monster became a lucrative commodity to be harvested with some profound, even catastrophic consequences.

The walrus has been hunted for the benefit of mankind for millennia, but only in the last few hundred years has this threatened the species' survival. To Arctic indigenous peoples, the walrus was, and for many remains, a staple food; a 1-ton animal that made a perfect 'meat-berg': food for humans and sled dogs and the raw materials for a range of essential manufactured items.[2] Hunting walruses was a dangerous and often fatal occupation, so much so that the Arctic explorer Elisha Kent Kane described the walrus as 'the Lion of the Esquimaux'.[3] For indigenous Arctic peoples the walrus's ferocity and intelligence gave it a potent symbolic role in shamanic religion; only the polar bear was more powerful. Skulls and tusks were used in rituals; powerful shamans could transform into walruses, and walruses could transform into shamans. Arctic peoples traded walrus products for thousands of years. Indeed, walrus ivory became one of the first global commodities, exchanged initially among indigenous peoples, but later sold by the Vikings, Russians and Bulgars to Europe, Persia, Arabia, Turkey and China. Walrus-hide ropes, possibly the strongest such material available until the invention of the steel cable, were rendered flexible by the application of walrus oil to provide the Vikings with the rigging for their longships.[4] Walrus rope may even have been used to hoist the stones of the great Gothic cathedral of Cologne.

Human activity limited the range of walrus populations somewhat, but prior to the beginning of commercial hunting, the walrus herds of the Arctic, sub-Arctic and more southerly latitudes probably numbered in the millions. It took large-scale exploitation by Europeans, beginning in the sixteenth century and peaking in

Indigenous walrus hunting, illustration from Elisha Kent Kane, *Arctic Explorations* (1856).

the nineteenth, to seriously endanger the species. While indigen - ous inhabitants made use of the whole animal, commercial walrus hunters sought only hides, oil and ivory, and not always all of these. Walrus tusks became low-value items sought after by sailors for carvings and engravings (or 'scrimshaw') to fill their idle hours, while machine belting from walrus skins formed a widely used component of the Industrial Revolution. Ivory and hide gradually became eclipsed by oil; for parts of the nineteenth century London and other large cities were almost entirely lit by the blubber of sea mammals. Unlike indigenous hunting with harpoons, commercial hunting with firearms was extremely wasteful; many more wal- ruses were killed than were recovered and used. Walruses were eradicated from many areas, leading to mass starvation among some indigenous peoples. Then, in the early twentieth century, marine mammal oil was largely replaced by mineral oil. There were no longer enough walruses left to make hunting profitable and, prompted by fears that the species would become extinct, protection measures were eventually introduced throughout the walrus's range.

The severed heads of walruses, hunted for their tusks by indigenous Alaskans, early 20th century.

Although it was for a time widely thought to be doomed, the walrus has bounced back beyond expectations in many areas. Tightly regulated subsistence hunting is now permitted only by indigenous peoples (although recently some of the quota has been sold on to big game hunters). But just as the walrus recovers from overhunting, climate change presents a potentially calamitous new threat. Uniquely adapted to life in the frozen Arctic, in a warming world the walrus's future is unsure.

Walruses live at the cusp of the most intricate and significant geopolitical issues of our time. Global warming not only threatens the walrus's habitat, but offers new opportunities for resource extraction in the Arctic that, given the lamentable environmental track record of the oil industry, for example, adds an extra level of uncertainty to the walrus's prospects. At the same time, the longstanding tension between the interests of Arctic indigenous peoples and the economic and political ambitions of industrial nations unavoidably involves walruses too. Environmental and animal rights issues are part of this awkward balancing of priorities. In our delicate ecological moment, should indigenous people continue hunting marine mammals as they have for millennia? If the political powers decide not, does this mean that conservation operates as another form of colonialism? To think seriously about walruses is to think about some of the profoundest and most intractable questions of modern history, and at the same time to think about one of the most curious and alluring of our animal relatives.

Long ago in the Arctic, there was a giant girl named Sedna with an insatiable appetite. She grew far bigger than her parents. She kept on growing and kept on eating until she even tried to eat her parents' legs. In desperation they took her out in the family canoe and threw her overboard, only for Sedna to seize the boat and to

A model walrus carved from walrus ivory by native Alaskans, possibly for the tourist trade, 19th century.

rock it until it seemed certain to capsize. Fearful for their lives, Sedna's parents cut off the fingers of one of her massive hands. The severed fingers, the tale goes, turned into animals: one a whale, one a salmon, one a seal and one a walrus. Thereafter Sedna lived at the bottom of the sea and became a potent figure deserving of great reverence: the goddess of the sea mammals.

This story of the origin of the walrus in the life of the sea goddess Sedna exists in various forms throughout the Arctic. The goddess is usually depicted as a woman with a fish tail, like a mermaid, but in some traditions she also has tusks. Sedna, meaning 'she down in the sea', is the name used by the Inuit of Baffin Island; in Greenland, she is Nuriviq, or Nerrivik, the 'Food Dish', and to the Chukchi of Siberia she is 'Mother of Walrus'. It was seen as vital for hunters to appease Sedna with offerings: if she was displeased she would not send animals to be killed. The dearth of sea mammals in the Chukchi Sea at the end of the nineteenth century (due to overhunting by American whalers) was understood by local people to be a consequence of the goddess's anger at the breaking of one of her tusks.

Arctic names for the walrus appear to be onomatopoeic in origin. The Inuktitut (Inuit language) words *aivik* or *aaviq* and the Chukchi *rerke* mimic the barking call made by walruses. Dependent on hunting for survival and intimately familiar with their prey, Arctic peoples have developed a complex vocabulary to describe animals of the same species but of varying age, size and even behaviour. To a hunter, a walrus resting on the ice is a different matter entirely to a walrus in the water. The Yup'ik people of St Lawrence Island in the Bering Strait (home to the town of Savoonga, which proudly declares itself the 'Walrus Capital of the World') have over 100 words for walruses and walrus products. In other languages the names of the walrus most frequently originate in the languages of the indigenous walrus hunters of Northern Europe, inhabitants of Scandinavia and northwest Russia.

When working on the 'w' definitions for the *Oxford English Dictionary* in 1919, J.R.R. Tolkien was particularly tested by the

Pacific walruses on an ice floe in a rapidly warming world.

entry for 'walrus', a word of both ancient origin and complex etymology. The current English word is first recorded in the seventeenth century and derives from the Dutch 'walrus'. This probably originates in the Old Norse *rosmhvalr* (horse-whale), which later became *hvalross* (whale-horse) in modern Norwegian. The first literary reference to the walrus appears in a ninth-century Old English account of the voyage of the Viking traveller Ohthere, commissioned (or possibly written) by King Alfred. Ohthere travelled from his home in northern Norway to the White Sea in Russia to see the world and hunt the walrus with the indigenous Sami people. He then journeyed south to England, presenting some tusks to the king. In King Alfred's account, the walrus is the *horshwael*, horse-whale again; the English of the Anglo-Saxons was closer to Old Norse and other Germanic languages than the modern version. Since walruses are not commonly found in

Female and juvenile Pacific walruses hauled out on the ice.

British waters, there seems to have been no further need for the word for many centuries to come, by which time the Old English *horshwael* reappeared as *morse*.

The Vikings were not the only people in Europe to hunt the walrus, and a parallel naming tradition evolved further east. The Sami called the walrus *morša*, which became морж (morzh) in Russian. The first use of 'morse' in English is recorded in William Caxton's *Chronicles of London* (1480), in which he describes the appearance of a walrus in the Thames: 'This yere were taken iiii grete Fisshes bitwene Eerethe and London, that one was called mors marine, the second a swerd fisshe, and the othir tweyne were wales.'[5] The Swiss naturalist Conrad Gessner uses both *morsus* and *rosmarus* in his great zoological work the *Historiae Animalium*, published in the 1550s. Latin was the language of scholarship, so the Russian морж became *morsus* and the Norse *rosmhvalr*, *rosmarus*. The Latin form *morsus* did not bode well for the reputation of the walrus – it is also the Latin for 'bite' and very similar to *mors* (death). Edmund Spenser uses a pun on *morse/mors* when describing an ominous sea monster in *The Faerie Queene*: 'The dreadful fish, that hath deserved the name/ Of Death, and like him lookes in dreadful hew.'[6] Sometimes *rosmarus* was used interchangeably with *morsus*, but in other instances it seems to represent a different creature. *The Faerie Queene* continues to list other sea monsters, concluding with 'greedy rosmarines with visages deforme', so to Spenser the morse and the rosmarine seem to be distinct. *Rosmarus* at least had more pleasant associations than *morsus* – in Latin *rosea* is pink and *mare* sea.

Until the nineteenth century, when the name 'walrus' became established, 'morse' or 'sea-horse' were the most common English terms for the animals. Unlike the creature we now call the sea-horse, the walrus does not seem to much resemble a horse, other than in its large size and herd behaviour. But it was perhaps not so much the appearance of walruses as the sounds they made that enabled the comparison. During a voyage to the Arctic in 1789, the writer and anti-slavery campaigner Olaudah Equiano encountered 'sea-horses', presumably walruses, 'which neighed exactly like any other horses'.[7] Vernacular names for sea animals were often maritime equivalents of familiar land creatures, following the ancient idea that all land animals had an aquatic equivalent; thus seals were sea-dogs, the killer whale was the sea-wolf and the porpoise the sea-pig or herring-hog. Some of these nomenclatures, such as sea-lion, elephant seal and leopard seal, survive today. These names were not always consistently applied to the same species; the sea-cow was the manatee and its extinct relative the Steller's sea-cow, but the term was also sometimes applied to walruses, as was sea-elephant. Other names for the walrus found in early European descriptions include *mo-horse, rohart* and *bête des grands dents*, the beast of big teeth.

The scientific name for the walrus is now *Odobenus rosmarus*, which loosely translates as 'the rosy sea tooth-walker': in fact this is quite a good description of the walrus, which can look very

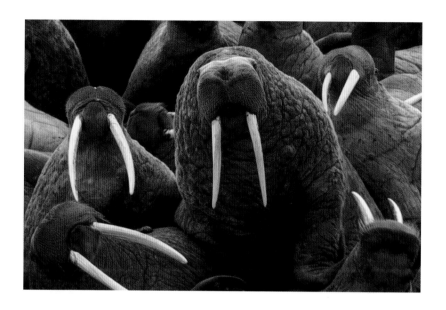

pink in warm weather when the blood flushes the skin to help the animal cool down. Early observers had correctly identified the walrus as a member of the seal family (although it was also classed as a fish, as was any creature that lived in the sea), and it was with the seals that it was placed when first classified as *Phoca rosmarus* by the great Swedish taxonomist Carl Linnaeus in 1758. Although there were many good descriptions of walruses, scientists were hampered by lack of access to actual specimens, being dependent on often poorly preserved body parts and the odd short-lived juvenile bought for a zoo. A considerable degree of confusion subsequently emerged within the scientific community about the origins of the walrus, and during the eighteenth and nineteenth centuries it was given a variety of scientific names, including *Trichechus rosmarus*, *Odobenus obesus* and *Rosmarus arcticus*. It was grouped for a long time with the manatee in the

Glowing pink walruses, an effect caused by blood flowing to the surface of the skin in warmer weather to help them stay cool.

A walrus with seals and a manatee, thought at the time to be close relatives; Gotthilf Heinrich von Schubert, adapted by W. F. Kirby, *Natural History of the Animal Kingdom for the Use of Young People* (1889).

genus *Trichechus*, and sometimes with even more unlikely relatives such as the anteater and elephant. In 1814 the anatomist Sir Everard Home concluded that

> The nearest approach to the walrus, is an animal found in the Indian Seas, with short tusks just appearing through the gums . . . The different species of manati appear, therefore, to be intermediate links between the hippopotamus and the walrus.[8]

In a later paper based on pickled body parts brought from the Arctic, Sir Everard described a similarity between the hind foot of the walrus and that of the fly, hypothesizing that the walrus uses suction cups on its flippers to enable it to walk on the slippery ice.[9] By contrast, the comparison with the manatee evidently has a sound anatomical basis. The front half of the manatee does resemble the walrus, and its relative the dugong (sometimes referred to as the 'tropical walrus') does have small tusks, but neither the manatee nor the dugong has any hind limbs. Yet the walrus has well-formed hind limbs and can walk on land like a quadruped. Once this was established, the walrus became the sole representative of the genus *Odobenus*.[10]

Specimens reaching European scientists were mostly of walruses from the Atlantic Ocean – Canada, Greenland or Spitsbergen – and Linnaeus described only a single species. The walrus of the Pacific Ocean is slightly larger and was first described as a separate species in 1811, based on specimens brought from Siberia by Russian ivory traders. Captain Cook's description of walruses encountered during his voyage to the Bering Strait in 1778 led a third species, *Trichechus cookii*, to be proposed in 1831, but these proved also to be Pacific walruses. In fact, there is today only one species of walrus, divided into two subspecies, the Atlantic walrus (*Odobenus rosmarus rosmarus*) and the Pacific walrus (*O. r. divergens*). It has been suggested that the walrus population of the Laptev Sea in Russia forms a third subspecies, but recent studies indicate that these walruses are probably a Pacific walrus population.[11]

A curiously shaped early depiction of an Atlantic walrus, based on Frederik Martens, *Voyage to Spitsbergen* (1675), reproduced in J. A. Allen, *History of North American Pinnipeds* (1880). Note the seal-like hind flippers.

Early Western image of the Pacific walrus, based on a drawing made during Captain Cook's voyage to the Bering Straits. Charles Heath, engraving in George Shaw, *General Zoology or Systematic Natural History* (1800).

The seal group, Pinnipedia (meaning feather-footed), comprises more than 30 species divided into three families: the Phocidae, earless or true seals, such as the commonly found grey and harbour seals and the massive elephant seals; the Otaridae, eared seals, such as sea-lions and fur seals; and the Odobenidae, walruses. The walrus is a 'relict' – sole survivor – species. Although there is only one species today, there were once many more and they may have been among the most numerous of the seals. Walruses share features with both the eared and earless seals: they do not have external ears, but can walk using their hind flippers like a sea-lion rather than drag their hind limbs behind them as a true seal does. Biologists debated for many years as to whether walruses were more closely related to the eared or earless seals, but the consensus is now that they are closer to the eared seals.

Pinnipeds evolved from bear-like carnivores, probably in the Arctic region, with the earliest pinniped fossils dating from the Oligocene period, around 23 million years ago.[12] The first tuskless proto-walruses emerged later in the Miocene era, around 10–12 million years ago, in the California area. The earliest walruses had no tusks, but they did have sharp teeth, possibly for fish-eating. Later species developed skulls and jaws evolved to the distinctive 'squirt and suck' feeding method, whereby the animal squirts jets of water to uncover food on the sea floor, then sucks the prey from its shell. Fossils of at least twenty species of prehistoric walruses have been found; some resemble modern walruses with tusks on the upper jaw, but others have no teeth apart from tusks, and the impressive *Dusignathus* walruses have both upper and lower tusks. The species thrived, diversified and spread from the North Pacific into the North Atlantic via the Central American Seaway between North and South America. Early fossil walruses have been found as far afield as Virginia and Japan, and they were probably the dominant pinniped of the Pacific for millions of years. At some point walruses may have become extinct in the Pacific Ocean, which was then repopulated by the Atlantic species, or they may have remained in the Pacific and evolved further. It

Gomphotaria Pugnax, an archaic four-tusked dusignathine walrus, artist's impression by Stanton F. Fink, 2007.

seems most likely that modern walruses first appeared around 5–8 million years ago in the Atlantic Ocean and spread back to the Pacific via the Arctic Ocean. Formerly they lived much further south than they do today – fossils have been found in Belgium, England and South Carolina – and may have been a temperate species that adapted to Arctic conditions. Around 600,000 years ago the cooling climate caused the Arctic sea passages to close and Atlantic and Pacific species to become permanently separated and subsequently to evolve independently.

The legacy of centuries of commercial hunting by European whalers means that today there are many more walruses in the Pacific Ocean than the Atlantic. Pacific walruses are found in the Bering Strait region, around the coasts of Alaska and eastern Siberia and in the Chukchi Sea.[13] They are migratory, so it is difficult to calculate population numbers, but scientists have estimated the population at around 200,000.[14] Pacific walruses cover huge distances, possibly up to 3,000 km (1,800 miles) per year, with the females travelling further than the males. Walrus herds, even very large ones, can be entirely composed of animals of only one sex. Every year, female and juvenile Pacific walruses migrate through the Bering Strait, following the ice south in the autumn and north in the spring. They follow the southern edge of the pack ice, swimming or sometimes hitching a lift on the floes. Summers are spent in Siberia, around Wrangel Island and the Chukchi Sea, winters in the southern Bering Sea. Male herds migrate less; some follow the females through the Strait, but others remain in the same areas all year round so that large herds of male walruses can be found on the islands around Alaska in summer. Laptev Sea walruses are an isolated population of around 4,000–5,000 that move only around the area of their home sea.

Atlantic walruses also migrate, although not such distances as their Pacific cousins. Today they can be found in the Hudson Bay area of Canada, the coasts of Greenland, the Arctic island groups of Svalbard, Franz Josef Land and Novaya Zemlya, and the coasts of Arctic Russia eastwards to the Kara and Barents Seas. Numbers, again, are uncertain, but there may now be as many as 18,000–20,000 Atlantic walruses. Their previous range was much more extensive; a large population once existed in the Gulf of St Lawrence (northeast Canada), and may have extended as far south as New England; they were also found in Finnmark (the northern coast of Scandinavia), Southern Greenland and Iceland. One medieval account describes walrus hunting in the Orkney Islands, and numerous sightings have been recorded in the Hebrides, Scotland and Ireland, most recently on the Orkney island of North Ronaldsay in 2013. Indeed, despite their relatively confined distribution, both Pacific and Atlantic walruses have a marked tendency to wander, or perhaps simply to get lost, appearing outside their normal range in areas as far south as Spain and Japan. In 1981 a stray walrus reached the English east coast and was airlifted back to the Arctic from the seaside town of Skegness after swimming the Great Ouse river in Norfolk. Their range appears to be limited by temperature. Walruses are generally very uncomfortable in temperatures above 10°c (50°F). Naturalists observing a walrus that travelled around the coasts of France and Spain in 1986 noted that it shivered, possibly indicating that a skin disease was causing it to feel cold despite the hot weather.[15] Male Pacific walruses that remain all year in the south Bering Sea often get too hot on land and take to the sea to cool down.

The walrus's extraordinary appearance has provoked wonder, horror or bafflement from generations of visitors to the far North. Vast walrus herds emit a truly remarkable stench and make for a striking first impression, one that the English sea captain Jonas Poole greeted with amazement on encountering walruses on Spitsbergen in 1604. Sending a boat to investigate, the crew feared

After arriving unexpectedly in a Norfolk garden in 1981, 'Wally the Walrus' was transported back to Greenland and released back into a more familiar habitat.

for their lives when a walrus emerged from the sea 'making a horrible noyse and roaring' so that those 'in the boate thought he might have sunke it'. A few days later they came across the rest of the herd: 'it seemed very strange to us', Poole reported, 'to see such a multitude of monsters of the sea lye like hogges upon heapes'.[16] As much as it is walruses' herd behaviour that provides such a notable sight, the immense size of individual animals also adds to the spectacle. The walrus is the second largest member of the pinniped family – only male southern elephant seals are larger. Male Pacific walruses can be up to 3.6 m (12 ft) long and weigh 1,700 kg (3,748 lb). Females are considerably smaller: up to 3.1 m (10 ft) long and 1,250 kg (2,756 lb) in weight. Atlantic walruses are slightly smaller than Pacific ones. Historically likened to an ox or an elephant, a full-grown walrus is nowadays most often compared in size to a mid-range family car. Although they are large, as bottom feeders walruses are not generally fast swimmers like other seals, but if in danger can manage a sudden turn of pace, both on land and in the water.

Since big bodies retain more heat, the walrus's ample dimensions are a significant advantage in the Arctic cold. Their internal organs are proportionally large; one biologist has described the forked veins that drain the walrus's lower body as so enormous that a man can draw them over his legs like a pair of trousers.[17] These physiological adaptations allow the walrus to survive the cold and withstand the water pressure when diving. Walruses can dive to depths of 100 m (328 ft), staying underwater for up to twelve minutes before needing to take a breath. They have sparse

Louis Agassiz Fuertes, 'Pacific Walrus', in Edward W. Nelson, *Wild Animals of North America* (1918).

fur even when young and adult males may be practically bald, so they depend on a thick layer of blubber beneath the skin for warmth.[18] This blubber can be up to 15 cm (6 in) thick, and comprise up to a third of the walrus's total body weight. Blubber not only insulates the walrus against the extreme temperatures of the Arctic but provides a reserve of fat to enable survival without food in times of scarcity. The walrus's distinctive wrinkly look allows free room for girth expansion; only the very fattest walruses lack wrinkles. It may even be that the walrus's skin folds form a unique pattern, like a fingerprint.[19] Visitors to London's Horniman Museum can, however, see a wrinkle-free walrus. When this specimen was sent to be stuffed in the late 1800s, little was known about walruses and the taxidermist stuffed the skin to its fullest extent, unaware of their appearance in the wild. This gives the walrus a somewhat inflated look, as if it might float away like a Pink Floyd pig, although this has not affected its appeal for visitors.

The famous Horniman walrus, stuffed to bursting point.

Walrus skin is very thick; it can be between 2 and 4 cm thick on the neck and shoulders, offering vital protection against stray tusks in the close quarters of the haul-out. A single walrus skin can weigh 178 kg (392 lb) by itself. Male walruses also have warty lumps on the skin of their necks and shoulders known as bosses or tubercles, which might either be a secondary sexual characteristic, or, alternatively, simply scars from fighting.

Perhaps the most distinguishing aspect of the walrus's appearance is the tusks. These occur on both males and females, and grow throughout a walrus's life. Rare individuals have more than two tusks and as many as five have been observed. A layer of dentine is added for each year of life, so the animal's age can be calculated by counting the rings in the tusks. Pacific walruses have larger tusks that tend to curve inwards and can meet at the tips; Atlantic walrus tusks are smaller and point outwards. The tusks of male walruses are heavier and thicker, but those of females can be longer, growing up to 1 m (3 ft) long. For many years the purpose of tusks was thought to be digging for food on the sea floor, but observation of healthy, tuskless walruses revealed this to be false. In fact, tusks seem to have a primarily social purpose. Tusk size indicates status in the social hierarchy for both male and female walruses; a walrus with missing or broken tusks has low status in the herd. Scarred and occasionally one-eyed walruses reveal the danger of a tusk stab in the fearsome (though seldom fatal) fights of males in the mating season. Tusks are also important in the gentler matter of clearing a path through the massed bodies of the haul-out. The absence of tusks can occur through a variety of factors: they can be knocked out in fights, lost by tooth decay or broken on the rocks – captive walruses often have their tusks removed because they become damaged on the sides of their concrete tanks. The walrus also uses its tusks to haul itself out of the water, anchor itself to ice floes and maintain breathing

A walrus with its vibrissae, or moustache, clearly shown, James Murie, *Transactions of the Zoological Society of London* (1869–72).

holes in the ice. They also function as weapons against other species, to defend against predators or occasionally attack large prey such as seals or even small whales. No other seal has tusks; most other seals hunt fish so require a mouth that can open widely, preventing the evolution of restrictively large teeth. Walruses do not have so much of a challenge to catch their main food of bottom-dwelling molluscs. For them the problem is finding and opening their meals.

Walrus eyesight is poor, and the sea floor is murky and obscured by sediment, so walruses search for food by touch using flippers, snout and whiskers. A recent study of handedness (flipperedness?) in walruses has revealed that most walruses favour the right flipper when searching the sea floor during feeding. Some 89 per cent of walruses are right-flippered, about the same proportion as humans.[20] Once the food is found, the walrus squirts the mud away and then sucks the mollusc out of its shell using the distinctive 'squirt and suck' feeding method. Early observers were puzzled by how walruses managed to live on shellfish, but had no shell pieces in their stomachs; however the suction mechanism of the walrus mouth is both strong and precise. Not only can they extract a mollusc from its shell, but in captivity they have been observed to suck all the flesh from a fish, leaving a perfect skeleton behind. They can even suck the paint from the walls of their tanks.

Walrus whiskers, or vibrissae (the original walrus moustache), are used to distinguish food from other materials on the sea floor. They can grow very long, but are worn down by use; hence wild walruses sport neat moustaches, while captive walruses sometimes end up with bushy clumps. Vibrissae are found in all seals and sea-lions, plus many other animals such as cats and dogs, but in walruses they achieve an unusually high degree of sensitivity. Walruses have 600–700 individual vibrissae, more than most other whiskered animals, and can move them as a group for general searching or individually, like chopsticks, to pick up small objects. In the Netherlands, a captive walrus was trained to accurately distinguish between 3-mm-thick circles and triangles using only its vibrissae. The walrus was blindfolded and would nod when a circle was presented and shake its head for a triangle. If uninterested in participating, the walrus could leave the session, and the scientists who designed the study reported that the walrus's attentiveness improved the more difficult they made the tasks.[21] The walrus biologist Francis H. Fay commented that the use of the whiskers and snout pad by walruses in captivity 'were at least as effective as two hands in sorting, selecting, and manipulating materials'.[22]

The efficiency of their feeding mechanism allows walruses to find and consume up to six molluscs a minute, and, given their size, walruses need a lot of molluscs. An adult walrus can eat 6,000 shellfish a day, and it has been calculated that the Pacific

'Rambling Rosie', a 70,000-year-old Late Pleistocene fossil of an adult female walrus found on Vancouver Island, Canada, in 1979.

walrus population eats 3.2 million tons of molluscs per year. The walrus foraging method produces distinctive troughs in the sea floor. Fossilized furrows in rocks dating from the Pleistocene period have been identified as marks left by the feeding of ancient walruses. These troughs were not made by indiscriminate feeders, however. Examination of stomach contents reveals that rather than hoovering up everything in their paths, walruses are quite picky eaters, using their vibrissae to select certain favourite species and disregarding others. Although primarily subsisting on clam-type molluscs, walruses also eat fish, crustaceans and octopi. A small minority of walruses have been reported to consume larger prey, killing and eating seals, small whales such as the beluga and even baby walruses. These 'rogue' walruses, nearly always males and lone hunters, are held in indigenous traditions to be orphans who were never taught how to eat molluscs by their mothers. Most walruses probably only resort to such a diet in times of dearth; the Danish author and explorer Peter Freuchen describes walruses leaping on to the ice as indigenous hunters are flensing narwhals: 'raging with hunger, they will flop along to meat and blubber and eat them, even if there are people standing three steps away.'[23] The proportion of entirely 'carnivorous' walruses has been estimated at 0.1 per cent and these animals have a distinctive appearance, being generally slimmer and with tusks stained yellow from blubber. Eating these walruses can be dangerous to humans as they may carry the parasite which causes the potentially fatal disease trichinosis, an outbreak of which (traced to infected meat) killed 33 people in Greenland in 1947.

Walruses are the most gregarious of mammals, hauling out onto land or ice floes to rest in herds that even nowadays, with the population reduced from its peak, can number up to 14,000 animals. They are highly tactile, constantly seeking contact with their fellows. Pacific walruses tend to gather on ice rather than land to be closer to their main food supply. The movement of the ice can also take them in the direction of their migration. Atlantic walruses, on the other hand, prefer beaches, with some notably unhygienic results. Freuchen observed that 'the walrus is a most uncleanly beast when lying on land, spraying its fellows with excrement and complacently wallowing in it'.[24] As with

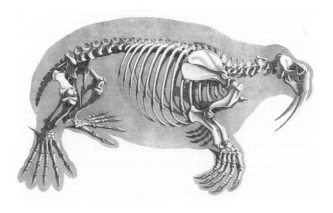

A walrus skeleton, engraving from Christian Heinrich Pander and Eduard d'Alton, *Die Vergleichende Osteologie* (1826).

Three views of the
head and tusks of
the Pacific walrus,
J. A. Allen, *History
of North American
Pinnipeds* (1880).

land-based herd animals, stampedes can cause younger and smaller individuals to be crushed. But, on the plus side, piling up in large herds keeps the walruses warm in the Arctic weather, and helps with locating mates and in defence against predators. Other than man, polar bears and killer whales are the only animals to threaten the walrus. While the herd sleeps, a small number of 'guard' walruses keep a look-out for danger – an essential task, as a sleeping walrus can be very hard to wake. Walruses sleep so deeply that some observers have assumed them to be either dead or inanimate boulders. According to a recent study, walruses have extremely unusual sleeping patterns. They sleep very deeply on land for long periods, but can also sleep floating vertically in the water, or even grab forty winks when completely submerged, and can go up to 84 hours without sleeping at all.

An Atlantic walrus contends with a polar bear, L. Lloyd, *The Game Birds and Wild Fowl of Sweden and Norway* (1867).

Even when the weather is not cold (by walrus standards), walruses group together and seek physical contact, exhibiting

The young Lord Nelson and his men fend off a walrus attack, illustration from D. Murray Smith, *Arctic Expeditions* (1880).

strong communal bonds. There are many sailors' accounts of walruses retaliating en masse when one individual is attacked. The zoologist Thomas Pennant wrote of walruses in 1784 that

> They are strongly attached to each other, and will make every effort in their power, even to death, to set at liberty their harpooned companions. A wounded Walrus has been known to sink to the bottom, rise suddenly again, and bring up with it multitudes of others, who united in an attack on the boat from which the insult came.[25]

Social position within the herd is maintained by threat displays and vocal communication. Walruses are extremely vocal animals both in and out of the water; hauled out herds can be detected a long distance away by the deafening noise as well as

34

the dreadful stench. They also communicate through facial expressions, often using their vibrissae to indicate emotions and status within the herd: raised vibrissae, for example, indicate submission to a walrus of higher rank. Like other seals, walruses often greet each other with the distinctive 'pinniped kiss', touching vibrissae nose to nose. This may enable each walrus to assess the health of the other or re-establish communal attachment.

Since walruses spend much of the year out at sea, beyond the reach of humans, many aspects of their lives remain mysterious. Residents of the Arctic Circle may frequently encounter polar bears – on the Svalbard archipelago it is unsafe to leave the town without a gun – but walruses are hardly ever seen. Walrus sex lives and breeding patterns have long been a subject of debate. They are not monogamous, as early European observers believed; nor do they have a highly polygamous 'beach-master and harem' breeding pattern, as do other pinnipeds, notably the elephant seal. Male walruses compete to attract mates by performing for the females: swimming in repeated patterns and singing to them, a courting ritual unique among pinnipeds. A single walrus song can last for days and carry for up to 16 km (10 miles). The songs' complexity has been compared to that of the humpback whale, consisting of a huge variety of sounds, including grunts, whistles, snorts, neighs and barks, created using the lips, tongue, teeth and nose. Most distinctively, the walrus can produce a rhythmic knocking and bell-like ringing using an inflatable pocket of skin in the throat. These pharyngeal pouches were thought to be only found in male walruses, but captive females have been discovered to have them too. Although female walruses do not sing during courting, trained captives have proved as able to vocalize as males. Mate selection is slightly different in Pacific and Atlantic walruses; the female Pacific walrus selects her preferred male based on the beauty of his song. In the case of Atlantic walruses, females have less choice: the male will perform for a small group of females and will mate with all of them. Both male and female walruses have sexually fertile periods, which do not always coincide. When apart from females, all-male herds hauled out on beaches have been observed to indulge in 'orgies' of mass homosexual behaviour.

After mating (during winter), the implantation of the fertilized egg is delayed for four to five months, giving the walrus a gestation period of fifteen months. This ensures that the calf is not born in the inclement winter months, but in the more favourable conditions of the following spring. Consequently, female walruses only mate at most every other year, resulting in a low birth rate compared with other pinnipeds. A high proportion of walrus calves do, however, survive to adulthood as walruses invest a great deal of maternal care in their offspring. Young walruses remain with their mothers for two to three years, longer than any other seal, while the walrus is the only pinniped in which males take any role in the upbringing of the young – males do not help raise their offspring, but will protect endangered calves.

Many observers have reflected on the mother walrus's extraordinarily diligent care for her offspring. Captain Cook noted that:

> the female will defend the young one to the very last, and at the expence of her own life, whether in the water, or upon the ice. Nor will the young one quit the dam, though she be dead; so that, if you kill one, you are sure of the other.[26]

More recently, scientists fitting walruses with radio tags in order to study their migration patterns were able to secure numerous males, but only one female subject. The walruses were first shot with a tranquillizer dart, but the females did not remain unconscious long enough for the tags to be fitted, leading to the hypothesis that the terrified barking of the surrounding calves woke the females despite their drugged state.[27] Unusually among mammals, orphan walrus calves will sometimes be adopted by other females. If separated from the herd, orphaned calves will seek assistance from any vaguely walrus-like object, including humans. One of two orphaned walrus calves successfully reared by the Alaska Sealife Center in 2012 was rescued after trying to climb into a fishing boat. In an account from the 1970s, the filmmaker Jacques Cousteau described how he and his team captured a baby walrus orphaned during an indigenous hunt. The young creature immediately bonded with the crew, becoming 'instantly and wildly attached'. Later, with the calf still on board, the boat was charged by a group of aggressive walruses. Just as they were about to strike, the calf cried out and the walruses immediately abandoned the attack. Cousteau was assured by his native guides that walruses never attack a boat if it is carrying a baby walrus.[28]

The tendency of mothers and other unrelated walruses to attempt to rescue the young if the herd is attacked was cruelly exploited by Southern walrus hunters. The nineteenth-century Scottish sport hunter Sir James Lamont describes the gruesome practice of attracting adult walruses by the capture of a 'junger' (walrus calf). Getting the calf in the boat, the hunters then commence 'stirring it up' (presumably beating it) with a harpoon butt:

> now the junger begins to utter his plaintive grunting bark, and fifty furious walruses close around the boat in a few seconds, rearing up breast high in the water, snorting and blowing as if they would tear us all to pieces.[29]

For all the brutality of his enterprise, Lamont also strikes a poignant note in depicting the emotions of his prey:

I don't think I shall ever forget the faces of the old walrus and her calf as they looked back at the boat! The countenance of the young one so expressive of abject terror, and yet of confidence in its mother's power of protecting it, as it swam along under her wing; and the old cow's face showing such reckless defiance for all that we could do to herself, and yet such terrible anxiety as to the safety of her calf![30]

A walrus calf is used to lure adult walruses towards hunters, P. Lackenbauer after Biard, in Alfred Frédol, *Le Monde de la Mer* (1866).

Images like this unavoidably evoke a strong response. Fay considers the bond between adult and calf walruses to have 'remarkable anthropomorphic implications'.[31] To the poet Robert Southey, the emotional life of the walrus was linked to its human appearance. Describing a walrus encountered by the young Horatio Nelson, he concluded that: 'As no other animal has so human-like

A mother Pacific walrus and calf, exhibiting their remarkably strong bond.

an expression in its countenance, so also is there none that seems to possess more of the passions of humanity.'[32]

Indeed, walruses are highly intelligent animals; possibly the most intelligent nonhuman inhabitants of the Arctic. Little research into walrus cognition has been carried out in the wild, but captive animals have provided some intriguing data. Orphaned calves rescued and raised by humans quickly become habituated to people, appearing so tactile and affectionate that they cannot later be released back into the wild. Numerous accounts of orphaned baby walruses being kept as pets testify to their adaptable nature. A walrus presented to King James I of England in 1608, for example, was described as 'of strange docilitie, and apt to be taught, as by good experience we often proved'.[33] There are limits, however, to what walruses may learn from human trainers, as scientists working at the Six Flags Discovery Kingdom in California discovered when they unsuccessfully sought to breed from their small Pacific walrus group. In captivity male

A. Radclyffe Dugmore, Walruses on an ice floe, 1914.

walruses are highly sexual, but not always discriminate in their attentions (one possible reason why other seal species often appear unwilling to share their tanks). In fact, the male walrus of Six Flags seemed more excited by power tools and recycling bins than by female walruses. By designing a training programme based around a prosthetic walrus vagina, the scientists were able to successfully collect semen samples and synchronize the fertility cycles of the male and female walruses, but sadly the subsequent pregnancy ended in a stillbirth.[34]

This same group of walruses has been used as test subjects in some surprising research into pinniped musicality. Folklore has long held pinnipeds to be musical; seals in Scotland were reputedly attracted by church bells, and Inuit hunters sang ritual songs to summon walruses. One recent observer has reported that hauled out walruses on a beach would approach him curiously if he sang to them. When trained to do tricks for animal shows in aquaria, captive walruses easily learn to perform movements and vocalizations on command. In 1884 a 'talking' walrus toured the U.S.; on signals from his keeper, he would say the words 'dog', 'cat' and 'boy', although the *New York Times* reported that 'it required a pretty fair stretch of the imagination to believe it a successful imitation'.[35] Captive walruses appear to be keen participants in educational programmes, exhibiting eagerness to begin sessions and frustration when unable to complete challenging tasks. The California research focuses on walrus vocalization, encouraging the animals to make as many different sounds as they can.[36] Until relatively recently, it was believed that animals vocalize only instinctively, and are not able to modify their sounds according to circumstance. However, although in the wild walrus songs are thought to be performed only by males and appear to be fairly formulaic, in captivity both male and female subjects learned to innovate and produce a variety of sounds in a way that might approximate to what we think of as 'creativity'.

Scientists in the expanding fields of ethology and comparative psychology are working to understand the emotions, behaviour and even cultures of the strange others with which we share the planet. The development of such branches of zoology is relatively recent, and can be controversial: the question of animal emotion remains hotly debated. However, the Western scientific tradition is only the most recent human attempt to understand the nature of the walrus. A far more intimate knowledge of these improbable creatures is perhaps most powerfully revealed in the world of the precolonial Arctic. Both the body and spirit of the walrus formed a central component of indigenous cultures that evolved over millennia in close relation to the animals with which they shared an often forbidding environment.

2 Walruses and the Indigenous Arctic

For ancient indigenous northern coastal communities, the hunting of sea mammals was the most essential of tasks, without which existence would simply not have been sustainable. Walrus hunting dates back many thousands of years; walruses were part of the fabric (both literally and metaphorically) of many Arctic cultures. The possible uses of the walrus are remarkably extensive, but the importance of walruses to indigenous Arctic peoples also exceeded mere use value, as material culture, cosmology, religion, myth and oral literature blend together to illustrate their significance as far more than resources.

Among his extensive research on northern peoples, Knud Rasmussen, an early twentieth-century Danish ethnographer who was himself part Inuit, reports a story from Greenland that illustrates a difficulty in piecing together the early human history of the Arctic:

> Our forefathers have told us much of the coming of the earth, and of men, and it was a long, long while ago. Those who lived long before our day, they did not know how to store their words in little black marks as you do.[1]

It was not until 1760 that the first Inuktitut script was devised by missionaries, and another 160 years or so after that before the written word was to become more or less universally adopted. What we know in the south of ancient Arctic cultures comes from a combination of oral narrative and the archaeological record, and later the accounts of sailors and explorers. Due to efforts to 'culturally assimilate' indigenous peoples during the nineteenth and early twentieth centuries through the suppression of traditional practices including ceremonial storytelling, a good deal of knowledge about the Arctic seems likely to have been lost. However, where it survives, oral tradition is remarkably accurate. An elderly Inuit woman interviewed in the 1860s was able to describe in detail the visits of the English explorer Martin Frobisher to the Arctic nearly 300 years before.[2]

Archaeological evidence of human habitation in the Arctic Circle has been dated back some 28,000 years in Russia's far north. This appears to have been a period of significantly more temperate climate prior to a notable cooling that pushed these early humans back down to lower latitudes. It was from the east that the North American Arctic seems to have first been settled, probably around 14,000–12,000 BC, by people crossing a bridge of land, long since vanished, linking Russia and America at the Bering Strait. The first residents of the American Arctic were not the direct ancestors of the present-day indigenous peoples. As in other regions, populations were not static; groups moved, new people arrived and communities died out or were assimilated into others. The millennium between 3000 and 2000 BC saw the rise in North America of Palaeo-Arctic (alternatively described as Palaeo-Eskimo) cultures, the first of which is now known by the distinctly unglamorous title of the Arctic Small Tool tradition (or AST₁), posited from tools (yes, small ones) found in Eastern Alaska. Their tools were small because as nomadic hunters they travelled light. Excavation of their middens reveals that AST₁ people hunted a variety of land and sea animals, including walruses. In Palaeo-Arctic societies, ivory was an important material for the manufacture of tools and cultural artefacts. A striking miniature mask, or maskette, carved of walrus ivory 3,500 years ago gives an eerie glimpse into the world of its Palaeo-Arctic artist, possibly a shaman, and is the oldest representation of the human face found in Canada.

The next significant staging post in the development of Arctic culture is the appearance of the Dorset people, originating around 500 BC. This culture is named after Cape Dorset in Nunavut, northern Canada, where the first distinctive archaeological traces of these people were found in 1925. To the later Inuit, the Dorset people were known as the Tuniit, or, alternatively, the Sivullirmiut (first inhabitants). It was the Inuit, or more accurately their ancestors the Thule people, who superseded the Tuniit, migrating eastwards from Siberia circa AD 1000. Here they had formed what is now referred to as the Old Bering Sea culture, aided by another rare period of relative warmth in the Arctic. The Tuniit were also maritime hunters, and are remembered in the Inuit oral tradition as being particularly skilled at hunting walruses. According to the Iglulingmiut of the Canadian Arctic, the Tuniit were so strong that they could break a walrus's neck with a harpoon line and pull along a walrus as easily as an Inuk does a seal ('Inuk' or person is the singular form of 'Inuit', which means 'people').[3] What survives of the Tuniit today is their art, much of which was created for religious purposes. Like the Inuit, the Tuniit followed a shamanic religion, using amulets, fertility symbols, masks and other ritual objects, often carved from ivory. Unlike seals, which are usually depicted naturalistically, walruses and polar bears are often stylized, indicating that they were spiritually the more powerful creatures. Their successors, the Thule culture, produced a decidedly different art, more abstract and less closely linked to shamanism.[4]

The Tuniit became extinct round about 1500, probably pushed out by climate change and pressure from technologically more advanced rivals. The Inuit subsequently became the predominant group of the North American Arctic. There is some difficulty in using 'Inuit' as an umbrella term for Arctic indigenous peoples, as it often (erroneously) occurs today. The Yup'ik of Alaska and Eastern Siberia and the Inupiat of Alaska's North Slope, although also descended from the Thule, are distinct ethnic groups from the Inuit of the eastern North American Arctic. While 'Eskimo' is a term rejected in many regions for its colonial associations, it remains in usage by indigenous peoples in parts of Alaska and Siberia as a convenient generic designation that expresses cultural difference from the Inuit. These peoples speak a variety of connected languages of the Eskimo-Aleut group, but there are many dialects and not all are mutually comprehensible.[5]

A mechanical doll's head carved from walrus ivory, Savoonga, St Lawrence Island, late Thule culture, c. AD 1000–1200.

If this history reveals a degree of diversity among Arctic indigenous peoples, there is also a close affinity between them: hardly surprising given the common origins of many groups and similar ecological conditions across the Arctic. Vegetation is sparse in Northern latitudes: in summer, cloudberries, crowberries and lingonberries provide three of the few sources of non-animal nutrition. Otherwise, survival traditionally depended on meat. For all the hardship that might be expected to go hand-in-hand with life in the Arctic Circle, visitors were often surprised by the relative comfort that the indigenous inhabitants managed to live in, testimony to an advanced culture that unfortunately still did not prevent many southerners from writing scathingly about northern peoples in terms of the racial hierarchies of the colonial era.

There is a notable irony to an article in the *London Reader* of 1881 that begins by asking of the walrus, 'What earthly service can such an ungainly, stupid beast render?'[6] The answer, in short, for indigenous peoples, is: food, clothing, rope, heat, light, tools, building materials (for boats and housing), hunting equipment, musical instruments and more. In locations of relatively meagre resources, an animal of the walrus's considerable dimensions constituted a real bounty. Every part of the walrus was valuable. With walrus hide used as a covering for traditional dwellings in many parts of the Arctic, usually stretched over a frame of whale ribs, and windows fashioned from stretched walrus gut, or sometimes penis membrane, a good proportion of time was spent living, in a sense, inside a walrus (the stereotypical northern accommodation of the igloo, built from snow, was restricted to the central Canadian Arctic). In the coastal Alaskan northwest, semi-subterranean dwellings made primarily of earth have also been observed in archaeological and early photographic records, often featuring walrus skulls as part of the exterior wall.

Walrus intestines were also made into waterproof clothing, and the lamps that provided heating and lighting were often

Edward S. Curtis, walrus hide stretched to dry on a frame, c. 1929.

46

fuelled by walrus blubber. Peter Freuchen described the manu-facture of the *ayayut*, a kind of drum which he calls 'the only Eskimo instrument', made from 'the skin of a walrus throat stretched over a frame of bone to which a handle is attached'.[7] There is also evidence of the use of walrus stomach or bladder as the heads of these drums. Walrus tusks were crafted into knives, sled runners, snow goggles and hunting visors, and also into an unusual implement consisting of a tusk split into two with a drilled hole at the end which appears to have been used as an early form of ear trumpet for listening for seals beneath the ice. Walrus shoulder blades made snow shovels, whereas walrus penis bones, which are often several feet in length, made good tent poles, a handy walking stick known as an *osik* or a useful wedge for an axe. Whiskers could apparently be used as nose-pickers and there is even an account of a walrus rib being used as a false leg.

Since a good deal of the summer was spent travelling, tents, again frequently of walrus hide, were a necessary component of

Traditional Chukchi walrus-skin houses, illustration from W. H. Hooper, *Ten Months Among the Tents of the Tuski* (1853).

Arctic life. The traditional form of locomotion for coastal peoples
was the *umiaq*, a kind of boat in common use throughout the
Arctic and an essential item for moving to hunting grounds. Like
housing, the *umiaq* was structured around a whalebone frame
(or occasionally a frame made from driftwood) that was covered
with the stretched skin of a walrus or bearded seal. A boat of
around 12 m (40 ft) in length would require the skins of three
walruses. The skin of the female walrus was preferred, as that of
the males is scarred from fighting and may not be waterproof.
One *umiaq* could service around ten people, so a considerable
harvest of walruses would be required to manufacture and keep
in repair the *umiaq*s needed for a single Arctic village. Walrus
hides were also used for the smaller, more manoeuvrable kayaks
('kayak', along with 'anorak', is one of the few Inuktitut words to
have entered the English language). If wood were in short supply,
hides could serve as the frames for sledges when rolled up and

frozen. Frozen blocks of walrus meat could be used to make a one-way eat-as-you-go sledge, as a convenient way of transporting food for dogs or people. The sole of a *mukluk*, a traditional Inuit and Yup'ik boot, was manufactured from the skins of young walruses, as was rope used for harpoon lines. Trampolining is an Arctic invention: tossing one another on a walrus skin was a popular game played at festivals in the Bering Strait region. Given their versatility, walrus hides were a common item of trade between Arctic peoples. The walrus, then, was a ubiquitous part of Arctic daily life; human existence was built around the walrus and other large mammals. And, of course, there is a lot of eating in a walrus.

Arctic cuisine is a sophisticated and culturally complex practice requiring expert knowledge of cuts and combinations of

A walrus skin *umiaq,* early 20th century.

meat and intricate preparation methods, including freezing, stuffing. pickling, fermentation (or, as some southern observers have put it, 'decomposition': a process known in Greenland as *mikiak*) and 'boning-out', the last a method for removing the bones of a seal while leaving the skin whole that resembles the galantine technique of classic French gastronomy. Similarly a dish known as *akutuq* (from the Inupiat word 'to stir') made from whipped reindeer and seal fat has been compared to a mousse or soufflé, although with added summer berries it is more commonly referred to as 'Eskimo ice cream'. Walrus meat is fibrous and strong-tasting, and many parts were reserved for dog food, especially the hide, although that could also be consumed by humans in an emergency. Frederick Schwatka, an American explorer who visited the Iwillik people of Hudson's Bay in the late nineteenth century, survived on walrus hide for many days, comparing the experience to 'eating a wire hair-brush'.[8] The parts of the walrus most valued for human consumption include the tongue, heart and flippers, and the contents of the walrus's stomach. As Freuchen explains: 'The stomach is always the prize portion, since it is usually filled with the most delicious clams and oysters, and the stomach juices serve as a tantalizing sour dressing.'[9] Fermented walrus meat, known by southern travellers as 'walrus cheese', was also a part of the Arctic diet, while walrus blood mixed with fat and added to greens and berries forms a purée (or *kashi*) eaten by the Chukchi.

Some dishes, such as *qongulaq*, walrus liver pickled in seal oil, take years to mature. Freuchen describes the recipe and the piquant result:

> They pickle walrus liver in a bag of blubber, keeping all air away from the liver. They suspend the blubber bag in a stone cache or cave for a year or more. It must not touch the

ground, and the sun must not reach it. When it is ready to be eaten the liver is green as grass, and tastes like strong, hot curry.[10]

A native Alaskan trampolining on walrus skin, early 20th century.

Pickled walrus flippers, known by the Inupiat as *utniq*, is another dish requiring considerable patience: the flippers are coated in walrus blubber, sealed in walrus skin and left to marinade for a year. Among the most relished of Greenlandic dishes is the *giviak*, 'the most festive food a Polar Eskimo can treat you to' in Freuchen's words. A recipe for this delicacy even made it into a chapter on freezing in a classic American cookbook, Irma S. Rombauer's *The Joy of Cooking*, though there is more than a touch of colonial irony in her description of the preparation of the dish:

Kill and eviscerate a medium-sized walrus. Net several flocks of small migrating birds and remove only one small

'The Walrus of Bering Sea', illustration from Henry W. Elliott, *The Seal-Islands of Alaska* (1881). 'The forms of Rosmarus struck my eye . . . in a most unpleasant manner.'

wing feather from each wing. Store birds whole in interior of walrus. Sew up walrus and freeze. Then two years or so later, find the cache if you can, notify clan of a feast. Partially thaw walrus. Slice and serve.

'Simplicity itself', Rombauer concludes, baffled and amused, far distant as she is in 1950s America from the traditional cultures of the North.[11]

Despite the technical refinement of Arctic cuisine, many colonial visitors were quick to grumble about the food, and walrus meat in its various forms was apparently among the items least likely to set the mouth watering. Henry W. Elliott's account of Alaskan foods in 1886 is particularly uncompromising:

I can readily understand, by personal experience, how a great many, perhaps a majority of our own people, could speak well, were they north, of seal-meat, of whale 'rind', and of polar-bear steaks; but I know that a mouthful of fresh or 'cured' walrus-flesh would make their 'gorges rise' . . . in fact, it is the worst *of all* fresh flesh of which I know.[12]

As Elliott's complaint implies, much colonial discomfort focused on the method of preparing meat, or perhaps more precisely the failure, in southern terms, to prepare it adequately. The derogatory usage of the term 'Eskimo' is often traced to what is now thought to be a mistaken etymology: 'eater of raw meat' from the Algonquian and Cree languages (the more likely derivation is connected to the lacing of snowshoes). Consuming raw meat was used as evidence of 'barbarism' in European and American accounts of Arctic peoples. Charles Francis Hall, who lived among the Greenland Inuit in the nineteenth century, felt that 'the Esquimaux custom of feasting on uncooked meats is highly repulsive'. Although he became accustomed to, and even relished, Inuit food, Hall always regarded it at best as the result of difficult circumstances and felt that a white man in the North would always initially be 'nauseated with every thing he sees and smells'.[13]

In fact, the technique known as *quaq*, by which meat is frozen and then partially defrosted, has recently been described by the Alaskan food writer Zona Spray Starks as 'one of the Arctic's greatest culinary achievements'. *Quaqqing* is a method that can be used on a wide variety of meats. Starks writes particularly appreciatively about walrus liver *quaq*, which, she explains, 'not only cracks between the teeth but also makes the mouth tingle and fizz at the same time'. The preparation of *quaq* is an elaborate and lengthy process instead of the primitive act of culinary debasement colonial commentators identified. Starks provides a detailed account:

Cut out the liver right away, when walrus is killed. Cut away bile, all of it. Soak liver in water, the ocean's salt water . . . Cut into pieces . . . Put in a pot, cover with water, bring to the boil. Don't boil; simmer . . . five, ten minutes. It should be rare. Cool in water. Change water every day until no more blood gets into water. In five days, maybe six, liver gets a little sour. Drain it. Put in cold cellar to freeze. When ready to eat, cut thin slices, dip in seal oil.[14]

Rather than being mere uncooked meat, *quaq* is an elaborate way of preparing animal protein that has been refined over centuries.

Not all southern travellers were quite so dismissive of Arctic food as Elliott and Hall. Schwatka, for example, gave a more upbeat account of the native diet:

The flavour of the walrus is almost identical with that of the coarser clams. This is not surprising, since in North Hudson's Bay he derives his main sustenance from these salty bivalves, for procuring which his villainous-looking tusks seem especially designed. I think I cannot better describe the walrus flavour and meat, than by citing the illustration of tough Texas beef, marbled with fat, and soaked in clam-juice. I think the two would be so near alike, that it would take an Eskimo to distinguish between them. To many this meat seems to be extremely repulsive; but much of this distaste lies in the imagination, and can be overcome in the same way that is done by the frog-hater, who eats frogs as birds, and then imitates Oliver Twist.[15]

Schwatka also wrote (almost) approvingly of a dish of walrus flippers, noting that 'leaving out a slight walrus flavour, they are not unlike a dish of pickled pigs feet, served hot'.[16] His enjoyment of the local food did have its limits, however. The contents of a walrus's stomach were a delicacy that he 'never starved enough' to try.

Unavoidably there is a degree of irony in the complaints of some southerners about the 'barbarous' native cuisine of the North. While indigenous food was nutritionally well balanced, the diet of preserved foods that sailors and explorers hoped to survive on was often insufficient to the task. The disappearance of Sir John Franklin and his crew of 128 on a mission in 1845 to discover the Northwest Passage through the Arctic Ocean to the Pacific is a prominent case in point. After decades of searching, it finally emerged that the party had all succumbed to disease or starvation, and may have been poisoned by their tinned food. The last survivors even, to the shock and disbelief of Victorian Britain, resorted to cannibalism. Of course, the most immediate nutritional danger to those unused to Arctic survival was the risk of scurvy. Fresh sea-mammal meat is an excellent anti-scorbutic: a fact well known to Arctic peoples. On an expedition in 1853 the American Elisha Kent Kane and his party began to suffer from the lack of vitamin C, a circumstance that Kane, a surgeon by training, attributed to 'our civilized diet'. 'Had we plenty of frozen walrus,' he observed, 'I would laugh at scurvy.' Saved by 'walrus beef' and *awuktanuk* (raw walrus liver with blubber) brought to them by the Inuit, Kane came to have a high regard for the meat, recalling 'the frost-tempered junks of this pachydermoid amphibian as the highest of longed-for luxuries'.[17]

Sailors, however, were notoriously conservative in their diets, and often refused to eat local foods, even to save their own lives. One early pioneer in the battle against scurvy was Captain James Cook. On his voyage to the Bering Strait in 1778 Cook came across a herd of walruses, ordering a number to be shot for food. Although Cook pronounced walrus-flesh 'sweet as marrow', when the meat was served to the crew instead of their usual salted rations they sharply disagreed, announcing it 'disgustful' and 'rank in both smell and taste'. Many refused to eat it, or were subject to 'purgings and vomitings' if they tried. Cook was enraged, calling his men 'damn'd mutinous scoundrels who will not face novelty', but was forced to restore the salt rations. According to Cook's biographer Richard Hough, enforced rations of walrus meat brought Cook 'nearer to suffering a mutiny than at any time in his career as a commander'.[18]

Later Arctic expeditions ensured greater success by adopting native methods: smaller parties travelled by dogsled with Inuit guides rather than ships with large crews to feed, and living off the land as opposed to bringing preserved rations. Walrus meat became the preferred dog food for exploring parties. When Robert Peary set out on his attempt to reach the North Pole in 1908 he took with him 49 Inuit, 226 dogs and the meat of 40 walruses. An Arctic-style diet even came to be recommended for its health benefits by those outside the North. Consisting almost entirely

Captain Cook hunting 'sea-horses', illustration from John Webber, *Cook's Voyage to the Pacific* (1784).

'Hoisting a Walrus to the Deck of the *Roosevelt*', Robert E. Peary, *The North Pole* (1909).

of meat, and including large quantities of animal fat but almost no fruit or vegetables, such a diet is very much out of step with current nutritional advice. There was no 'five-a-day' for the Inuit, yet they appear to have been remarkably healthy. The Polar Inuit of Greenland rarely suffered from southern ills such as heart disease, tooth decay or cancer before Europeans introduced processed foods.

The vital importance of walruses to the Arctic way of life illustrates the cultural centrality of hunting. Killing a walrus was no easy business, and was surrounded with a good deal of ritual and prestige. Walrus hunting required extensive organization to ensure that, in the words of the Yup'ik of Round Island, the kill was *cakarpeknaki*, which is to say, respectful to the animals and without waste.[19] Freuchen reports the renewed respect he was held in after killing his first walrus: 'I was "newborn in the land" – as the natives put it – because harpooning a walrus is the first step toward becoming a hunter. I was *somebody* now.'[20] Killing animals was seen as a form of respect; it was believed that animals that were not hunted would not thrive, and would decline in number.

Traditionally, hunting at sea was undertaken from a kayak (indeed, kayak means 'hunter's boat'), using a harpoon. Since the harpoon's range was extremely limited, the walrus had to be engaged at dangerously close quarters. Unlike hunting with guns, in which animals could easily be fatally wounded but lost to the hunters, harpooning meant that when an animal was hit it was very likely to be secured. Once the walrus was struck with the harpoon, the wounded animal would make a prodigious effort to escape. In summer hunts an inflated bladder (made from a whole seal skin) attached to the end of the line enabled hunters to track the fleeing walrus. Walruses were prone to attack these floats, although not apparently (according to the people of Baffin Land and Hudson's Bay) if a newly born lemming was placed inside the bladder. Getting close enough to the walrus on the open ocean to throw the harpoon required a good deal of skill, with the hunter needing to judge in the first instance where a walrus would be likely to next surface. The walrus was too intimidating an opponent for a single hunter, so walrus hunts were usually communal efforts. Once a hunter had successfully harpooned a walrus, his colleagues would rally round for the kill

Indigenous walrus hunting at sea, recorded by engraving onto ivory tools, Walter J. Hoffman, *The Graphic Art of the Eskimos* (1897).

and finish it off with spears or clubs. When killed at sea, the carcass would need to be inflated lest it sink and be lost. This was done by inserting a tube into its stomach and blowing it up like a balloon, making it easy to tow to land for butchering.[21]

In winter, when sea-ice made this method impractical, seals and walruses were hunted from the ice at their breathing holes. This form of hunting required a great deal of patience as hunters waited for an animal to return. As the walrus was so strong, the harpoon line ended in a noose coiled around the hunter's neck, which would be looped over a spike rammed into the ice as soon as the walrus was speared. This was extremely dangerous. Charles Francis Hall observed this hunting method in Greenland, and remarked on the 'recklessness and cool daring of the Innuit . . . for if he should fail to free his neck of the coil at just the right moment, he would inevitably be drawn headlong beneath the ice'.[22] Occasionally, a single lost walrus might be discovered stranded above the ice and away from the rest of the herd. Long walks in search of open water are a possible cause for a no doubt painful complaint occasionally suffered by male walruses: a fractured penis bone.[23] Such unfortunate animals, in Greenland called *paunguliaq*, were easy prey for hunters, although often in a poor condition, deprived of access to their food on the seabed. Given the opportunity, indigenous people were able to dispatch walruses in quantity. In the shallow bays near the mouth of the Kuskokwim River in Alaska Yup'ik hunters in kayaks would assemble in a line between group of walruses and the sea, and by shouting and banging their paddles drive the animals ashore, where they could be more easily killed.[24]

Mishaps, it seems, were far from uncommon. The celebrated Norwegian explorer Fridtjof Nansen relates a story from Greenland

in which a hunter's kayak was attacked by a walrus from below and 'a long walrus-tusk was suddenly thrust through its bottom, through the man's thigh, and right up through the deck'.[25] Hunting young animals was a particularly perilous enterprise given the strong familial bonds among walruses. It was also highly advisable to dispatch the walrus as quickly as possible: a wounded animal was very dangerous, could take hours to kill, and if it survived would be more aggressive towards humans in future.

Once the walrus had been killed, the considerable task of preparing, or flensing, the animal's body could take place. The task was tiring and time-consuming, and hunters sustained themselves by drinking the fresh blood of the walrus or eating slices of raw liver. The first step was the removal of the walrus's eyes so that its spirit would not see the butchering. Too large to be transported whole, the walrus would be cut up into manageable pieces. There was a strict order of priority in the partitioning of the walrus among the hunters. Franz Boas records that the hunter who first strikes the walrus receives the tusks and one of the fore-quarters; the second striker takes the second fore-quarter; the belly falls to the next in line and the hind-quarters

Walrus ivory harpoon and toggle, with rope of walrus sinew, Eskimo-Aleut, Alaska, 19th century.

to the two next.[26] Hunters (and their wives) were expert butchers. Preparation of the hide was a job for the women. Skins would first be soaked in sea water to remove blood, and then fermented to remove hair. The remaining flesh was scraped from the skin with an *ulu*, a semi-circular knife, and the hide stretched on a wooden frame. Thicker hides were carefully split in half lengthways to make them go further and be more flexible before drying.

Ritual forms an integral part of the preparation for, and the conclusion of, a walrus hunt. Any part of the walrus that is discarded is returned to the ocean, accompanied (as custom dictates) by *kunnikun* ('calm water'), a gift to sea creatures for which, in return, they might keep the seas calm. Oil drippings left around an ice-hole from which a walrus had appeared were said to encourage the walrus to return. Sometimes songs or incantations were performed to summon or placate the walruses. Taboos prevented hunting at certain times, such as after an illness or

'Plunging the Harpoon', illustration from Henry W. Elliott, *The Seal-Islands of Alaska* (1881).

bereavement. In Greenland, a hunter returning to the sea after a period of mourning had to use a special incantation to address Nuriviq/Sedna: 'Drive walruses towards me / Thou Food Dish down there / Below the ice! / Send me gifts!'[27]

Rigorous dietary taboos surround the preparation of walrus meat, many of which related to concern for the souls of the hunted sea mammals. If taboos were transgressed, pain would be caused to the animal's spirit, which was thought to endure beyond the body's death. Particularly, in the central Arctic, there was an interdiction on contact between the walrus and the caribou. Since these animals were both reputed in some traditions to have been created from the clothing of the same mythic woman, walrus and caribou meat needed to be kept strictly separate. When a walrus was killed on a hunt, a message was immediately sent back to the rest of the community in order to halt any work on caribou skins. Conversely, during the caribou hunting season, no walrus-related materials could be taken into the grounds of the caribou. There were also similar laws governing the contact between seals and walruses. According to Boas, the Inuit would

Kenojuak Ashevak,
Walrus Spirit, 1965,
colour stonecut
print.

Amulet made from walrus ivory, North American Arctic, 19th century.

always 'change their clothing or strip naked before eating seal in the walrus season'.[28] Neither would salmon be eaten on the same day as walrus. As Boas puts it, any transgressions of this kind would be 'fastened to the walrus's soul'.[29] Any soul offended in this way was described as a *tupilak*. These spirits were said to roam through the community causing difficulties as they tried to free themselves of the transgression visited upon them. Walruses that presented particular problems to hunters were often thought of as *tupilak*s. Boas reports a story from the Aivilik Inuit of Nunavut of a walrus with long hair 'like a person' that seemed intent on luring the hunters out to sea. However, it transpired that this *tupilak* was not created by the disturbance of an animal's soul through a failure of ritual, but by a neighbouring enemy who called the creature into being in order to destroy the hunters.

Religious observances reveal the conception of traditional Arctic hunting as an engagement with the animal's spirit, or *inua*, as much as its flesh. Appeasing the dead animal's soul meant that future hunts would have every chance of success. Animal behaviour was deeply meaningful in relation to social practices; animals responded, it was thought, to human actions in complex ways. A walrus dismayed at a Greenlandic family concealing a miscarriage, for example, reacted in dramatic style, grasping a man 'with his huge fore-flippers, just as a mother picks up her little child', and dragging him into the sea and trying to pierce him with his tusks before finally letting him go.[30] To the Inuit, if rituals were not correctly observed, or taboos were broken, Sedna would become too depressed to comb her hair. Sea mammals would become tangled in it, and would not come to the surface to be hunted. Given such potentially catastrophic responses from animals, relationships with sea-creatures needed careful attention. The key figure across the Arctic world in mediating between species, and between the spiritual and the physical world, was the shaman, or *angekkok*. Shamanism formed the heart of an animistic world view that pivoted on the inter-relationships between different life forms, and on the particular insights of a privileged being, the shaman, able to travel between the natural and supernatural realms.

To communicate with the spirit world, shamans used a special magical language. People, animals and hunting implements could not be referred to by their usual names, so walrus, usually *aaviq*, became *sitdlalik* in incantations. Perhaps the most vital aspect of the shamans' role was their relationship with Sedna/Nuriviq. The shaman was the intermediary between the goddess and mortals, transmitting her wishes and conveying human prayers. As one Inuit elder describes, 'shamans must swim down to the depths of the sea and comb Nuriviq's hair for her. And in her gratitude, she offers humankind all the creatures of the sea.'[31] In the Arctic, shamanism focused on the quality known in Inuktitut as *qaumaniq*, generally translated as 'vision', an experience in which the shaman was able to recruit the assistance of *tuurngait*, or helping spirits. Shamans could be either men or women and initiation followed lengthy training, often after a kind of apprenticeship to an existing *angekkok*. Rasmussen records the shaman Ava's account of his becoming an *angekkok* during a moment of 'great, inexplicable joy': 'in the midst of such a mysterious and overwhelming delight I became a shaman, not knowing myself how it came about. But I was a shaman. I could see and hear in a totally different way.'[32] The visual possibilities available to the *angekkok* unfold, as Rasmussen explains:

> as if the house in which he is suddenly rises; he sees far ahead of him, through mountains, exactly as if the earth were one great plain, and his eyes could reach to the end of the earth. Nothing is hidden from him any longer; not only can he see things far, far away, but he can discover souls, stolen souls, which are either kept concealed in far, strange lands or have been taken up or down to the Land of the Dead.[33]

These visionary powers aided the *angekkok* in a range of social functions: teaching, healing, exposing members of the community who broke taboos and directing hunters to their prey.

It was in the task of visiting Sedna/Nuriviq that a particular connection between shamans and walruses emerges. Many shamans were reportedly able to transform themselves into walruses in order to undertake the difficult journey to the Sea Goddess's home at the bottom of the sea. Frequently, the guardian spirits of an *angekkok* would include a walrus, or at least a being with the head of a walrus. Walruses were also central in the elevation of an *angekkok* from a lower to a higher grade of practitioner. In some parts of the Arctic, shamans were divided into those called an *ekungassok*, skilful but lacking in strength, and those known as a *poolik* who were consummate masters of their

Edward S. Curtis, Ceremonial maskette, Nunivak Island, Alaska, 1929.

art. The promotion in status from *ekungassok* to *poolik* hinged to a large extent on the shaman's relationship with bears and walruses. Henry Rink, who published a volume of *Tales and Traditions of the Eskimo* in 1875, reports that it was 'by being able to invoke or conjure a bear and a walrus' that a shaman became a *poolik*. After the bear has been conjured it seizes the shaman and 'throws him into the sea', whereupon 'the walrus, devouring them both, afterwards throws up his bones again on the beach, from which he comes to life again', transformed in shamanic potency.[34] Shamanic traditions had resonance beyond the Arctic. Norse mythology features numerous shape-shifting mages, and there is even a walrus transformation. In the fifteenth-century *Saga of Hjálmþér and Ölver*, an evil king pursues the heroes in the form of a walrus 'angry and frightful to behold'. The walrus king is defeated and killed by a warrior in the form of a swordfish and his own daughter in the form of a porpoise.[35]

While the shaman was thought to take the form of a walrus, the use of ritual spirit masks also made a figural connection, making the unseen world visible to the community. Walrus masks represented the spirit that allowed walruses to be taken by hunters and formed part of ceremonies involving dancing, drumming and storytelling. These masks' symbolism is often elaborate, and more than one animal might be depicted on a single mask. A mask from the lower Yukon showing a horned puffin eating a walrus reveals the spirit of a hunter acting through the bird and illustrates the close connection of different species and their spirits. In many cases, masks were made to reflect the dreams of shamans. Although there has been a considerable revival in the manufacture of indigenous Arctic artefacts since the middle of the twentieth century (and it is now a significant industry in the North), the identification of traditional masks as art is something of a misnomer. Indeed, the concept of art as a representation with a purely aesthetic, as opposed to practical function was introduced to the North by the *qallunaat*, or white colonizers; there is no word for 'art' in Inuktitut. There is, however, an extremely rich tradition of carving, especially associated with hunting equipment (hunted animals, it was thought, would much rather be killed by beautiful weapons), and other tools.

Walrus ivory was the material of choice for such work. Pictorial engravings on drill bows – put simply, a tool for making holes – formed one of the most prominent indigenous 'artistic' practices that later influenced the scrimshaw work of sailors. Preparing the ivory for such work was in itself a time consuming task. Once

Traditional tattoos and labret piercings, Kotzebue Sound, Alaska, Louis Choris, 1822.

the tusks had been removed from the skull, they were sliced lengthways along the grain. This was done by making a groove with a sharp stone along the length of the tusk, then carefully striking a blow so the ivory split as desired. The surfaces were then polished before carving or engraving. If the ivory was too hard, it could be softened by soaking in urine. Etching was done with sharp flints, and darkened with soot, blood and (latterly) gunpowder. Not only were these implements made from walrus tusks, but a significant proportion of them also represented walruses, most commonly in depictions of hunting scenes. Although no inhabitants of the Arctic ever developed a written language, such illustrations were used to record significant events and personal information. For example, a man might carve a picture of a walrus hunt in order to commemorate a famous exploit, or identify himself as a walrus hunter.[36]

These depictions were not restricted to tools and clothing, but extended to the body itself. Body modifications, such as tattoos and labrets (lip piercings), had the effect of making people resemble walruses. The labrets adopted by various peoples, mostly men, of the Bering Strait area were double piercings of the lower lip, widened by bone or ivory plugs resembling small tusks. It is not certain what the function of these were, but it may be that they served as a magical defence against walrus attack or served to transform the hunter himself into a walrus. Tattooing has an ancient heritage in the Arctic. Masks made by Palaeo-Arctic people thousands of years ago seem to show tattoos. Some facial tattoos resemble labrets and may have had a similar function. Women were also extensively tattooed, often with lines like whiskers on their chins and faces that may have been intended to imitate or attract animals.[37]

From children's toys to burial amulets, the image of the walrus, the spirit of the walrus and the walrus's body are ever-present in many Arctic coastal cultures. Walruses were even present in the Northern Lights, which were said to be the spirits of the happy dead playing football with a walrus skull. Explorers

Record-breaking walrus tusk, Pribilof Islands, Alaska, V. B. Scheffer.

describe arrangements of walrus skulls left on beaches or found in the landscape, ancient and moss-covered, like a walrus-head Stonehenge. Walrus heads had a symbolic function and were used in religious ceremonies. When the Russian explorer Mikhail Stadukhin encountered the Chukchi in 1647, he reported that 'they kill the walruses . . . and bring back the walrus heads with all the tusks and offer prayers to these heads'.[38] Nunivak islanders in Alaska held a walrus ceremony after hunting in which a walrus head was hung on the rear wall of the men's house facing the entrance. Gifts were brought to it, songs sung to it (imitating the voice of the walrus) and boys would pretend to hunt it with toy spears. After the ceremony, the head was taken outside and left on the beach to attract more walruses.[39]

Some elements of present-day environmental or animal rights movements have often been uncomfortable with, or even openly opposed to, traditional livelihoods, however ancient, structured around hunting marine mammals. It is important, of course, not to idealize Arctic indigenous peoples as living in a simplistic state of nature. Trade routes have stretched out of the Arctic for centuries; oral literatures recount significant social problems, often around domestic violence. Arctic peoples did not hunt 'sustainably' with a view to avoiding over-exploitation, although the many taboos restricting hunting may have had this effect. But perhaps the key note in thinking about ethics and walruses in the indigenous Arctic is the emphasis on the inter-connection between species. Significantly animals and humans were not considered by indigenous Arctic peoples to be funda-mentally different. Numerous stories exist of humans (and not just shamans) transforming into walruses. An elder from the Bering Strait, for instance, illustrated how his family tree came to include a walrus:

No 5. (1) Harpooning and lancing walrusses.

No 5. (2) Towing homewards the captured walrusses.

My great-grandmother came from a family where one of their members became a walrus . . . My grandfather told me that every time the walrus came south he went out with the walrus and went south. He did that several months every year. Until one day the walrus hair started growing on his body . . . And he told his family, 'I'm not coming back next year'. But they still heard him among the walrus, barking, calling his name.[40]

Sketch of indigenous walrus hunting, illustration from Henry Rink, *Tales and Traditions of the Eskimo* (1875).

A story from the Kivalliq region of Nunavut reveals an even more intricate sense of connection between human and walrus, explaining the transmigration of the soul through different animals. An old woman who died and was buried was eaten by a raven. Her soul passed into the raven. The raven was killed and fed to a dog, so the woman's soul passed into the dog, which was eaten by a wolf so her soul moved on again. The wolf fed on a caribou, only to be trapped and killed by a man, so the soul moved then into the caribou, but when that too was killed, her soul became a walrus, then a seal and finally a human again, who remembered her experience as other animals, and how as a walrus 'other walruses used to come up and kiss her until her nose became sore'.[41] Knowing ourselves as deeply connected to other species is a powerful ethical force that tempers human activity with respect for other beings. In the context of such respect, there is equality between species: human and walrus can learn from each other.

The relationship between a respect for cultural diversity that honours indigenous practices that have been marginalized and repressed since colonial contacts from the eighteenth century onwards, and a commitment to the ethical value of the lives of other species is one of the great ethical questions of our time. There is a danger, as many commentators have pointed out, that environmentalism becomes a form of neo-colonialism, with the South instructing the North what people there may or may not do. Any sense of ecological self-righteousness directed from the industrial South to the North is startlingly ironic, of course. The impact of colonialism in the Arctic on the lives of walruses and on the people whose lives were involved so closely with walruses reveals a horrifying story of violence and cupidity. As the shaman Sorqaq explained to Freuchen, 'The Great Nature is embarrassed by the white men who have come to live with us.'[42]

3 The War on the Walrus

Walrus ivory, oil and hides have long had a commercial value outside the Arctic, facilitated by extensive trading networks between indigenous peoples and out into the wider world. As well as being vital for the survival of maritime hunters in Greenland, Europe, Siberia and North America, walruses were valuable 'cash crops' that enabled the acquisition of goods that would otherwise have been unavailable. Trade fairs, tribal exchange, taxation and raiding brought walrus products into global trading networks where they passed from one merchant to another, often travelling far further than it was possible for individual humans to travel; further, indeed, than their ultimate purchaser's knowledge of the world extended. Walrus ivory came into the hands of artists and artisans in Europe and Asia who had no idea what a walrus looked like, or where it came from.

The Vikings are the first recorded commercial dealers in walrus products from outside the Arctic, although the trade was no doubt already ancient when it made its first literary appearance in the ninth-century account of Ohthere. Ohthere travelled around the north coast of Scandinavia to the White Sea in Arctic Russia, and reported to King Alfred of Wessex that 'he chiefly went thither . . . on account of the horse-whales (walruses), because they have very good bone in their teeth; of these teeth they brought some to the king; and their hides are very good for ship

Viking walrus
ivory belt buckle,
12th century,
found in Uig,
Isle of Lewis.

ropes'.[1] Although unable to hunt walruses at home in Norway, Ohthere seems to be familiar with the species, and aware of the hunting tradition in Arctic Russia.[2] Primarily associated today with violent invasion, raiding and other piratical activities, Vikings were also extensively involved in commerce. Even before the end of the Roman Empire, the ancestors of the Vikings were trading commodities from the North, notably amber, furs and slaves, to the markets of the South in exchange for coin and metal goods. During the Viking Age (approximately AD 780–1070), walrus ivory, hides and oil were among the goods traded by Norse merchants along two major North–South sea routes: the eastern route from the Baltic via rivers to central Europe and the Balkans, and the western route down the Norwegian coast to the North Sea and the rivers of Western Europe. Once transported south, walrus products and other goods would be sold or bartered in market towns. Demand for walrus ivory was high. Although elephant ivory was better quality for carving, it became hard to come by after the collapse of the Roman Empire broke down traditional trade routes. With the rise of Islam, Muslim-Christian rivalry continued to hamper trade with Africa. Walrus ivory filled the gap, and was traded as far afield as Spain, Constantinople and even Arabia.

The Vikings also made use themselves of the walrus products they dealt in, most notably walrus hide ropes for rigging and anchor ropes. The traditional way to make walrus hide rope was to skin the dead walrus in a spiral so that the longest possible unbroken strip of hide was removed. Once cured, the rope would be very stiff, but flexibility was ensured by the application of walrus oil, which would also aid waterproofing. A thirteenth-century description of the walrus by the German theologian Albertus Magnus records that such ropes were sold in Cologne market all year round.[3] Although latterly replaced by cheaper hemp ropes, walrus hide ropes were still being used by Norwegian sailors in the twentieth century. The builders of the *Dragon Harald Fairhair*, a modern-day Viking ship built using authentic techniques and materials in Haugesund, western Norway, hope to use walrus cordage for the rigging.

Norse colonization of Iceland and later Greenland provided another source of walrus products. Anticipating the effects of later European colonization, several walrus populations may have been eradicated as a result. Iceland has no walruses today, but there are place names and textual references indicating that a population once existed, and some walrus bones and ivory carvings have been discovered. Additionally, there appears to have been walrus hunting in the Faroes and in Scottish islands, also colonized by Vikings. Walrus bones have been excavated at Jarlshof, a Norse site on Shetland, while the Neolithic tomb at Maeshowe on the Orkney Mainland contains some revealing twelfth-century graffiti left by Viking treasure hunters. Much of it embraces the perennial themes of graffiti everywhere – 'Ottarfila carved these runes' and 'Ingigerth is the most beautiful of all women' – but there are also carvings of a dragon, serpent and walrus, although the walrus is rather shoddily illustrated (some scholars think it is not even a walrus, but an otter with a fish in its mouth).[4] Hector Boece's history of Scotland, first published in 1527, contains a rather surreal description of Orkney walrus hunting, probably derived from Albertus Magnus's earlier account. According to this, the walrus is taken when sleeping, moored by its tusks to the rocks:

At this time the fisherman cautiously approaches the sleeping animal and separates as much of its skin from the blubber near its tail as he can; into the groove he has separated he slips a noose of strong rope. Repeating the

A rope looped through a cut in a walrus's skin, in order (apparently) to flay the walrus alive, Olaus Magnus, *Historia de Gentibvs Septentrionslibvs* (c. 1555).

process with more ropes, he secures their ends to metal rings previously driven into the adjacent cliffs, or to powerful stakes driven into the ground, or to nearby trees. Then with the aid of a large sling he lobs stones at the walrus's head until he awakens the animal. The aroused walrus, in its frenzy to escape, tugs with its head and back against the restraining nooses and literally strips the skin from its tail. The self-wounded animal crawls away, but soon afterward is captured not far from its original location, floating on the water in a hopeless state of ex-sanguination, or lying half alive on the shore.[5]

It seems unlikely, to say the least, that a walrus could flay itself alive in this manner, but it is a traditional Inuit practice to pierce the skin of a dead walrus and thread rope through in order to more easily haul the carcass onto the beach for butchering, so there may be a remote factual basis for these accounts.

The Norse colony in Greenland survived for several hundred years, disappearing for unknown reasons around 1500. Colonists greatly valued familiar and luxury goods from home imported by visiting vessels. They made extensive summer hunting trips north to acquire walrus ivory and polar bear skins to exchange for these. Ivory was also used as currency; in 1327, 373 walrus tusks were sent from Greenland to Europe as tax payments to the Norwegian king and tithes to the papacy. The Norse Greenlanders did not eat walruses. Archaeological digs reveal that only the heads were brought back to the settlements in order for the tusks to be removed. Most of these tusks were then exported. One explanation for the failure of the Norse colony in Greenland is that it remained too attached its own traditions, preventing adaptation to its new environment. Had it adopted indigenous habits of hunting, clothing and diet it might have survived. Encounters between Norse and Thule people in Greenland appear to have been brief and violent but, in an interesting echo of shamanic religious practices, a number of tusked walrus and narwhal skulls were found on the site of the Norse cathedral at Garðar. Poul Nørlund, the archaeologist who excavated the site, commented that 'it is perhaps not impossible that religious or demonical ideas have been attached to these strange animals'.[6]

Native Alaskans hoisting a walrus carcass using a rope looped through the skin, illustration from Henry W. Elliott, *A Monograph of the Seal Islands of Alaska* (1882).

The Lewis Chessmen, c. 1150–75, walrus ivory and whales' teeth. Thought to have been made in Norway, these chess pieces were found on the Isle of Lewis, c. 1800.

The best-known surviving Norse walrus ivory artefacts are the Lewis Chessmen, discovered buried on the Hebridean Isle of Lewis in 1831 and quite possibly the world's most famous chess pieces, notable for their curious facial expressions. A few are made from whales' teeth, but most of the 78 pieces are carved from walrus tusks. They date from around 1150 to 1200, when Lewis was part of the kingdom of Norway and a hub of the trade route between the Norse homeland and its outlying colonies; similar pieces have been found in Ireland and Scandinavia. Probably made in Norway in the ivory-carving centre of Niðaros (Trondheim), they would have been high-value luxury items, and may have been hidden by their owner for safety. Their distinctive style has influenced modern children's fiction. The *Noggin the Nog* children's books and cartoons of the 1960s were inspired by the chessmen, as was the 'Wizard's Chess' game in the *Harry Potter* films.

The Bury Cross, probably carved in the 12th century from the tusks of a walrus that died in the 7th century.

Artists throughout Europe used ivory primarily for Christian devotional objects, such as crucifixes, reliquaries and croziers, but also for secular items such as gaming pieces and knife handles. Several centres of ivory carving grew up around the cathedrals and abbeys of England, notably Canterbury and Winchester. Intricately carved tusks were used to adorn churches, relics and prelates until the fourteenth century, when ivory became unfashionable. Many such pieces survive; one of the best-known is the so-called Bury Cross, famous as much for its romantic story as its fine workmanship. The cross came onto the international art market under mysterious circumstances in 1955. Despite a lack of

Walrus ivory Christ on a reliquary cross containing part of a human finger, Anglo-Saxon, c. AD 900–1000.

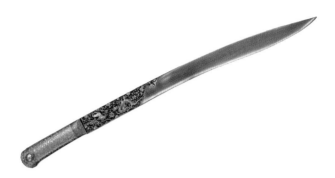

A 16th-century sword, from the workshop of Ahmed Tekelü in Istanbul, c. 1525–30, steel, walrus ivory, gold, silver, rubies, turquoise and pearls.

provenance, experts agreed that the cross was genuine, and was made in England during the twelfth century. It has been speculated that this is the long-lost cross of the abbey of Bury St Edmunds, Suffolk, carved in the twelfth century from a pair of ancient walrus tusks kept among other valuable items in the sacristy. It would be a fine story if the lost Bury Cross could be found after 700 years, but art historians disagree about this attribution.[7] Whatever its origin, carbon-dating has revealed that the walrus tusks from which it was made were at least 500 years old when the cross was carved, meaning that the walrus probably died sometime in the seventh century.

Most medieval walrus ivory originated in Russia, where walrus tusks (known in Russia as 'fish-teeth') were high-status items often given as gifts in diplomatic missions, as well as valuable trade goods. Tusks were traded in Asia by Russian, Chinese and Bulgar merchants, and a centre of ivory carving developed in Khiva in modern-day Uzbekistan. In the medieval Muslim kingdoms of Egypt, Asia and India, ivory of many kinds was used for making handles for knives and swords. The material most greatly prized for this purpose was known as *khutu*; not only did it make fine sword handles, but it was desirable as an alexipharm, a protection against poison. The myth of an alexipharmic horn probably originates with Chinese belief in the medicinal properties of rhino horn, which dates back at least to the fourth century AD and still threatens rhinos today. This myth spread to the Arab world and thence to Europe, and became intertwined with the myth of the unicorn, a magical creature whose horn also had curative properties. The true nature of *khutu* remains a mystery. It is sometimes described as the tooth of a fish from the northern seas, which has led some scholars to attribute it to the walrus, but also as coming from a bull, bird, snake or tree. The most recent theory suggests the frontal skull bone of the musk ox, another Arctic inhabitant.[8]

Walrus tusks were among many other materials commonly passed off as unicorn horn, but belief in their medicinal value persisted even when they were known not to be unicorn. A sixteenth-century English doctor given a walrus tusk brought back from the New World, for example, found it 'as soveraigne against poyson as any unicornes horne'.[9] Another medical use for the walrus is recounted by the twelfth-century abbess and mystic St Hildegard of Bingen, who in her *Causae et Curae* describes a cure for dimness of the eyes through the application of the dried skin of the 'fish called welra'. The skin should be softened in wine, wrapped in a cloth and applied between the eyes on alternate nights, but removed before midnight, the abbess advised.[10] By the seventeenth century, belief in unicorns, and in the medicinal value of the walrus, was not so widespread. Sir Thomas Browne, in his book of *Vulgar Errors*, lists the erroneous sources of the unicorn horn, including 'the tooth of a Morse or Sea-horse'. Walrus tusk for Browne 'Antidotally used, and exposed for Unicorns Horn . . . is an insufferable delusion', although he did concede that 'being burnt' it 'becomes a good remedy for fluxes'.[11]

As every schoolchild knows, when Christopher Columbus went looking for a sea route to Asia in 1492 he discovered that America was in the way. This was good news for European nation builders looking for new lands to colonize, but bad news for the people – and walruses – already living there. With the southern territories and sea routes dominated by Spain and Portugal, French and English explorers looked towards North America and the possibility of a passable Arctic seaway to Asia. This was the fabled Northwest Passage, the philosopher's stone of Arctic exploration for centuries to come, and the graveyard of hundreds of explorers. Less well known today, but equally fraught with hazard, was the Northeast Passage, heading to Asia the other way, north of Scandinavia and Arctic Russia. Although neither passage would be successfully navigated for hundreds of years, the search began the opening up of the vast Arctic regions to colonization and commercial enterprise. Unlike the Spanish and Portuguese colonies, the wealth of the North lay in living resources rather than gold and silver: fur-bearing ermine, beaver, sable, seal and fox; vast shoals of codfish; and whales, soon to become the most profitable of all.

Early accounts of travel to the northern seas are full of their authors' wonder at the numbers of creatures they found there. Long characterized as bleak and barren, the Arctic does not have the variety of species found in more southerly latitudes, but what creatures there are could be found in great numbers. Even to experienced sailors, many of these animals were completely new. Most would have been familiar with seals, but a herd of hundreds of walruses – massive, stinking and bellowing, with yard-long tusks and troubling red eyes – must have been a terrifying sight. They had never heard of or imagined such a thing: to such men the walrus was a genuine sea monster. The English explorer Sir Humphrey Gilbert and the crew of the *Golden Hinde* encountered a walrus off the coast of North America during a voyage of 1583. They didn't know what it was, but left an evocative description:

a very lion to our seeming, in shape, hair and colour, not swimming after the manner of a beast by mooving of his feete, but rather sliding upon the water with his whole body (excepting the legs) in sight . . . confidently shewing himself above water without hiding . . . Thus he passed along turning his head to and fro, yawning and gaping wide, with ougly demonstration of long teeth and staring eies, and to bidde us a farewell (coming right against the *Hinde*) he sent forth a horrible voice, roaring and bellowing as doeth a lion, which spectacle wee all beheld so farre as we were able to discerne the same, as men prone to wonder at every strange thing, as this doubtless was, to see a lion in the Ocean sea, or fish in shape of a lion.[12]

The walrus was lucky; unaware of its value, Sir Humphrey and his crew were content to marvel at the strangeness of the world and leave it unmolested. However, once accounts of the natural riches of the North Atlantic reached Europe, plans were set in train to harvest them.

Nowadays, the range of the Atlantic walrus in North America is limited to Eastern and High Arctic Canada, but in the past it extended down the coast of Labrador and Newfoundland past the Gulf of St Lawrence, and may even have reached as far as New England. The Gulf of St Lawrence is the world's largest estuary, and the coast and offshore islands offer the shallow seas, wide variety of mollusc species and sloping beaches ideal for walruses. When European colonists first arrived, very large walrus populations existed on Sable Island off the coast of Nova Scotia, Miscou and the Magdalen Islands in the Gulf of St Lawrence, Prince Edward Island and various other points in the Gulf. These southernmost walrus herds may have numbered in the hundreds of thousands, and were the first to attract the attention of adventurers.

The first colony in the region was established by the Portuguese in 1521, possibly in the Bay of Fundy. It was intended that the settlement should include a soap factory, which would traditionally have used lye (from wood ash) and fat, which in Portugal would have been olive oil. North America had no olives, so mammal oil made from the blubber of seals and walruses, known as 'train oil', was probably substituted. The Portuguese colony failed, but soon after the French established a more successful foothold. In 1534 the French explorer Jacques Cartier made the first of three voyages to the region, and brought back a description of a natural paradise, with islands 'as full of birds as any meadow is of grass' and more fish than had ever been seen or heard of before. He also left an unmistakable description of walruses:

> very great beastes as great as oxen, which have two great teeth in their mouths like unto Elephants teeth, and live also in the Sea. We saw one of them sleeping upon the banke of the water: wee thinking to take it, went to it with our boates, but so soone as he heard us, he cast himself into the Sea.[13]

The French began walrus hunting from their colonies in the Gulf of St Lawrence area in the sixteenth century, although few accounts survive of the fishery. In 1591 a French vessel, the *Bonaventure*, killed 1,500 walruses on the Magdalen Islands, but was captured by the English on its return journey, stimulating an unsuccessful English attempt to join the hunt. As train oil became increasingly valuable in the sixteenth and seventeenth centuries, industrial-scale walrus-processing plants were built by French colonists in several locations, notably Miscou Island. Walruses were killed here in their thousands. Men would approach the herds at night, wake them with loud banging and shouting, and drive the terrified creatures inland until they were exhausted and could be more easily slaughtered. So many were killed on Miscou that there are accounts of beaches composed entirely of their bones. By 1763, when the French North American colonies were taken over by the British, the walruses had been driven from many of their previous haunts. Concern for the future of the sea-cow (as walruses were then known) fishery led to the introduction of legislation to regulate walrus hunting in the colony of St John (Prince Edward Island) in 1770, but it was too late. British colonists were as eager for profit as the French, and under new management the licensed Magdalen walrus fishery was still taking as many as 25,000 walruses a year. After the Revolutionary War of 1775–83, unlicensed American fishermen from New England also began sailing to the Gulf of St Lawrence to hunt the walrus. By 1800 the last population was destroyed. Now they are largely forgotten, the only trace of their presence being a few place names such as Seacow Pond on Prince Edward Island.

Foiled in their attempt to encroach on the French-controlled walrus fishery of the Magdalen Islands, the English looked to acquire train oil elsewhere. The English Muscovy Company had sought a monopoly on whaling rights from Queen Elizabeth I in 1577, but whaling was a specialized profession, practised in Europe only by the Basques, so the company first sent ships to hunt the walrus. In 1591 the sea captain Thomas James of Bristol wrote a letter to Lord Burghley, the treasurer and trusted advisor of Elizabeth I, proposing such a voyage. He appended *A Briefe Note of the Morsse and the use thereof*, detailing the utility of walrus hides in making archery targets and explaining the value of ivory: 'The teeth of the sayd fishes . . . are a foote and sometimes more in length: and have bene sold in England to the combe and knife maker at 8 groats and 3 shillings the pound weight, whereas the

Benjamin Waterhouse Hawkins, 'Taking the Walrus', illustration from Thomas Varty, *Graphic Illustrations of Animals* (mid-19th century). The hunter is trying to blind the walrus, possibly with gunpowder.

best ivory is sold for halfe the money.'[14] Things began to look increasingly ominous for the walrus.

Walruses were plentiful in the territories of Spitsbergen (now known as the Svalbard archipelago), discovered in 1596 by the Dutch explorer Willem Barentsz during a voyage in search of the Northeast Passage. Uninhabited by man, Spitsbergen was another paradise for wildlife. Having never previously been hunted, the abundant populations of walruses, seals, whales, bears and seabirds had no fear of humans. Once the walruses were located, however, it initially proved difficult to kill them. An English expedition of 1604 encountered huge numbers of walruses on Bear Island, a small island in the Svalbard archipelago. They tried shooting them, but seventeenth-century firearms were no match for the thick skins and skulls of the walruses, and 'of above a thousand' only fifteen were killed.[15] Subsequent expeditions developed a more successful method using lances instead of guns. A description of the hunt was included in the journal of Robert Fotherby, a member of a voyage to Spitsbergen in 1613:

Theise morses use to goe ashoare upon some beach or pointe of lowe land, where the snowe doth soonest melt or dissolve; and ther will they lie upon the sand, close together, grunteing much like hoggs, and sometimes creeping and tumbleing one over another. They never goe farre up from the water-side: and therfore the men that goe to kill them strike theise first which are next the water, that their dead bodies maie be a hinderance to barre the rest from escapeing; for they all make towards the water, without anie feare either of man or weapon that opposeth them. Theise also are killed with launces which are verie broadheaded, to the end that they maie make the more mortall wound for the speedie killing of them, because they are so neare the water, and also manie in nomber; for, in some places, they will lie 400 or 500 morses all together. This sea-beast being dead, his teeth are taken out of his upper jawe; and his skin, or hide, is fleyed of him, first on the one side; and his fat or blubber, which lies next to his

Gerrit de Veer, Members of the Barentsz expedition attacking walruses with axes, illustration in Jacob van Heemskerck, *Reizen van Willem Barents* (1594–7).

skinne above his flesh, is also taken off: and then is his other side tourned up, and ye like againe done with it. Then is the blubber put into cask, and carried to the choppers; and by them it is chopped, and put into the coppers; and ther it is tryed, and reduced to oile.[16]

Using this method, hunters were able to kill hundreds of animals in a few hours, leading to the collapse of the Bear Island walrus population. Given the numbers of whales observed in Spitsbergen waters, it soon became apparent that more money was to be made from whaling than walrus hunting. Dutch and English merchants hired Basque whalers to teach their crews the necessary skills and the whaling trade began, initially based on Spitsbergen. The walruses of Spitsbergen continued to be hunted, but from the small boats of Russian trappers rather than large vessels.

By 1800 whaling had become one of the world's most lucrative trades. Many a fortune was made from the bodies of the

Samuel Purchas, after Robert Fotherby, 'The manner of killing ye Seamorces', 17th century. Walruses were driven inland and killed with lances.

leviathans, but it could not last; as time went on whalers had to
search longer and travel further to kill smaller whales. Arctic
whalers had always taken a few walruses if they found them and,
as whales became progressively more difficult to find, they began
to diversify with more determination rather than return home
empty, or 'clean' in the whaling parlance of the time. In the 1840s
the bowhead whale population of the Bering Strait was discovered by American sperm whalers, prompting an 'oil rush' to the
region by whalers of various nations. Arriving in the straits, the
whalers did not fail to notice the thousands of walruses hauled
out on the ice, but initially very few were hunted. An account of
the American walrus fishery in the 1880s explains the reasons
for this:

> partly because the whales were so plenty that they needed
> nothing else to help make up a cargo and partly through a

dread of these animals, of whose ferocity the men had read exaggerated accounts.[17]

At times, a degree of compassion among whalers also appeared in favour of the walruses. The historian John Bockstoce quotes an account of 1849 by the wife of a whaling captain who encountered a walrus that 'showed no fear and came close to the ship to look at it'. Since 'it looked so innocent he left it and was not sorry'.[18] But by the 1860s, with whales becoming ever scarcer and oil increasing in value, the whaling fleet eventually turned its attention to walruses in earnest. It was not practical to hunt whales in spring while ice cover was still extensive, so the ships filled up with walrus oil while they waited. Initially, the crews had the same trouble with developing techniques as their predecessors in the Atlantic: hunting walruses using methods honed on elephant seals proved unsuccessful. However, the introduction of rifles helped produce an extremely efficient method. Whalers would wear pale clothing and approach walruses downwind – walruses have poor eyesight but a good sense of smell – then pick off the animals one by one. As long as each walrus was shot dead immediately (so wounded animals would not bellow and panic the herd into retreat), an entire herd could be killed. Gunshots did not worry walruses, possibly because the sound is similar to the splitting of icebergs. By this method, hundreds of walruses could be killed in a few hours. A lot of walruses were needed to produce equivalent yields to whaling; 500 walruses could produce 300 barrels of oil, but 100–200 barrels could be extracted from a single bowhead whale. For the next twenty years, as whales continued to decline, more and more whalers turned to walruses until they too became too scarce to be commercially viable. Bockstoce has estimated that about 150,000 Pacific walruses were taken, mostly between 1869 and 1878, and that at least twice as many were killed as were recovered. This had devastating results for the human populations as well as the walruses.

Deprived of walruses and whales, some indigenous groups could turn to alternative food supplies, such as land mammals, but others, particularly those who lived on islands, were entirely dependent on maritime resources. If the walrus hunt failed, these people had nothing to fall back on, and starved. In Alaska a famine on St Lawrence Island during the winter of 1878–9 killed 1,000 people: two-thirds of the population. Many whaling captains were aware of the problem, as illustrated by this letter from a Captain Nye to the *New Bedford Standard* newspaper:

> I should like to see a stop put to this business of killing the walrus and so would most of those engaged in it. Almost everyone says that it is starving the natives . . . the people have eaten their walrus skin houses and walrus skin boats; this old skin poisoned them and made them sick, and many died from that.[19]

Another captain estimated that for every 100 walruses killed a family starved. Famines also occurred on the Russian side of the Bering Strait. The ethnographer Waldemar Bogoras records that the Ke'rek people were starving because the walrus has been driven from their waters. One of his Yup'ik acquaintances tried to reason with the whalers: 'Take the whales, but leave us the walrus. We also want something to eat. We shall give you all the walrus tusks.'[20] Although these whalers consented, it was not concern for the welfare of local people that ended the walrus hunt in the Bering Strait. By the 1880s there were so few walruses that the hunt was no longer commercially viable, and it was abandoned.

The story was similar in the Atlantic Ocean. Persecuted for many years, the bowhead whale populations declined and

whaling became unprofitable. New whaling grounds were sought as each became exhausted, with the whaling fleets of Britain, the Netherlands and other nations going increasingly further afield, from Spitsbergen to Greenland, Hudson's Bay and the Davis Strait. Whalers' goods became much more diverse as they struggled to find enough whales; for example, in 1900 the whaler *Diana* brought back from the Davis Strait 90 tons of whale blubber, 4 tons of whale bone, 54 walrus hides, three narwhal hides, eighteen seal skins, two hundredweight of walrus tusks, thirteen narwhal horns, 23 bear skins and one live wolf.[21] The Industrial Revolution had spurred demand for oil to be used in machine lubrication, textile manufacture and chemical processes. As well as being a valuable alternative source of oil, walruses were also useful for a variety of factory machinery. Once tanned – a process that could take several years – walrus hide made extremely strong machine belting. The Hull firm of J. H. Fenner even patented its walrus belting, and it was displayed at the Great Exhibition of

London in 1851. Other usages of the walrus hide included metal polishing, glue manufacture and billiard cue tips (there were even walrus skin banknotes, printed by the Russian-American Company for use in its American colonies prior to the Alaska purchase in 1867). By the 1890s a new market for walrus hide as the material for bicycle seats led to an increase in its price which stimulated trips concentrating on walrus hunting. Six hundred walrus hides taken by one Dundee vessel in 1897 fetched the considerable sum of £6,000.

Walruses were also targeted by seal hunters. Russia was particularly prominent in the trade in seal fur. Thousands of walruses were hunted on the Aleutian and Pribilof Islands, supplementing the highly lucrative fur seal industry. Hunting was largely done by indigenous peoples, paid and organized by the Russian-American Company. Between 1799 and 1867 as many as 10,000 tusks a year were being shipped west by the company. Peter the Great himself constructed a chandelier made entirely of walrus tusks, now in the Hermitage Museum. When Alaska was sold to the USA in 1867, walrus products were among the huge wealth of natural resources enumerated by U.S. Senator Charles Sumner in his speech on the cession of the territory. Popular opinion was not entirely on his side, however. Some newspapers mocked the

So-called 'walrus skin' money from Russian-America (c. 1800–1830), which was made from various materials, including seal skin or even parchment as well as walrus.

Benjamin Waterhouse Hawkins, 'Walrus skin for glue', illustration from Thomas Varty, *Graphic Illustrations of Animals* (mid-19th century).

Walrus skin for Glue.

proposed purchase as a waste of money, calling the region 'Walrussia' and imagining it composed of nothing but walrus-covered icebergs. As with whales, fur seals were overhunted, leading to the decline of the trade, but whereas conservation measures saved the fur seal populations of the Pribilof Islands, the walruses were eradicated.

The late nineteenth century saw train oil superseded by gas and kerosene. Alongside this, the value of walrus tusks declined to the extent that they were even used as ships' ballast. While ivory was much in use as umbrella handles, walking sticks and false teeth, this demand came to be largely satisfied by elephant tusks from European colonies in Africa. Unlike walrus tusks, elephant ivory is solid, so could be used for larger objects like billiard balls. With its commercial value on the wane, walrus ivory was increasingly used in scrimshaw work. This traditional art form, practised by American sailors in the eighteenth and nineteenth centuries, possibly had its origins in the indigenous ivory carving tradition. Sailors engraved walrus tusks, whalebone and sperm whale teeth with maritime and romantic scenes. As whaling declined, so did the whalers' art, although it was later popularized by President John F. Kennedy, who collected scrimshaw and often displayed it in the White House. The whaling

Painting commemorating the purchase in 1867 of Alaska with walruses in the foreground, oil on canvas, 1993–4.

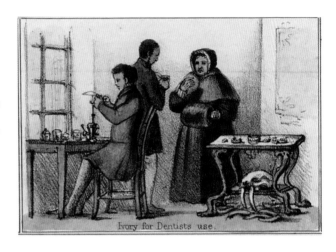

Benjamin Waterhouse Hawkins, a dentist crafting false teeth from walrus ivory, illustration from Thomas Varty, *Graphic Illustrations of Animals* (mid-19th century).

Ivory for Dentists use.

period also saw the development of a trade in items produced by indigenous carvers for sale to whalers, gold-diggers and other white visitors to the Arctic. Exposed to European influence, indigenous communities needed income to purchase goods such as guns, tobacco and alcohol. Walrus tusks carved with hunting scenes or made into cribbage boards became popular souvenirs. However, tourists did not always get what they paid for. Some tusks were exported to Japan by merchants, carved and then shipped back to Alaska to be sold as 'Eskimo' handicrafts. Similarly, an account of 1913 from Alaska describes walrus ivory being sold as elk teeth, prized by members of a popular North American fraternal order: 'Full many a member of the Benevolent and Protective Order of Elks is proudly wearing on his watch charm a tooth that had its original sphere of usefulness in masticating mussels, sea-grass and other food in the voracious mouth of a walrus.'[22] Once a unicorn, the walrus had become a deer.

The reduction in the value of walrus products did not spell the end of the war on the walrus. Arctic sport hunting became

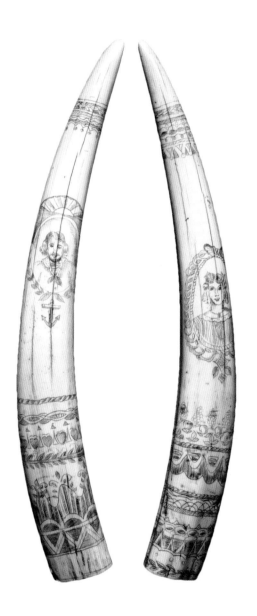

Whalers'
scrimshaw
made from
walrus ivory,
c. 1900.

Edward S. Curtis, a Nunivak ivory carver, 1929.

increasingly common in the late nineteenth and early twentieth centuries. Hunters included wealthy Europeans and Americans, but the British were prominent among them. Lord Tweedsmuir, son of the novelist John Buchan and sometime walrus hunter, wrote that 'in Britain we have probably carried the technique of sport to greater lengths of refinement than is to be found in any other country in the world'.[23] These hunters sought excitement and trophies; walrus heads, along with polar bear skins, were the most sought after. The Duke of Orléans, a big-game hunter and claimant to the French throne, visited the Arctic several times, writing in 1909 that 'The best of all trophies a hunter can bring back with him from an Arctic expedition is a walrus head. The possession of a fine bear skin may, indeed, be more desirable, but from the sportsman point of view the walrus is the true sporting animal of the North.'[24] Big-game hunting was by no means a male preserve; notable female hunters include Agnes Herbert, who went Arctic hunting with her cousin Cicely and wrote a book about the trip.[25]

The best-known Victorian walrus hunter was Sir James Lamont, MP for Buteshire, correspondent of Darwin and author of two popular books detailing his expeditions to the Arctic. After losing the election on his first attempt to enter Parliament in 1857, he embarked on a hunting expedition instead, later declaring

'WALRUS TEETH!' *Pacific Commercial Advertiser*, Honolulu, 1860. From Hawaii, walrus ivory was shipped to China and Japan for carving.

A walrus head mounted as a trophy. Agnes Herbert, *Two Dianas in Alaska* (1909).

that the result had 'proved unfortunate for the walruses, although perhaps the cynical reader may be disposed to add, "fortunate for the constituency"'.[26] He made several trips to the Arctic, eventually giving up his seat in Parliament to return to the North. Lamont considered walrus hunting the most exciting he had experienced:

> the more I see of walrus-hunting, the more keenly I enjoy it. It is a 'noble game.' It is like elephant-shooting, boar-spearing and a gigantic exaggeration of salmon-fishing all in one – thus combining three of the grandest sports to which mortal men are addicted.[27]

Although initially attracted by the excitement of the hunt, he took a keen interest in the natural history of the walrus, with an anthropomorphic approach to walrus behaviour that he often deployed to comic effect, as when describing this herd on an ice floe:

> I should think there were about eighty or one hundred on the ice, and many more swam grunting and spouting around, and tried to clamber up amongst their friends, who, like surly people in a full omnibus, grunted at them angrily, as if to say 'confound you, don't you see that we are full.'[28]

For all Lamont's bloodthirsty enthusiasm, sport hunting was an elite pastime practised by relatively few people, and as such probably had little impact on walrus populations.

Although by 1900 the Arctic whaling industry was defunct, it was to come roaring back with the invention of the exploding harpoon gun by the Norwegian whaler Svend Foyn which enabled the killing of the faster rorqual whales (including the blue, grey and humpback whales). Commercial walrus hunting also

How to hunt a walrus, according to Gilpin Lovering, 'a sportsman of wide experience', in E. Marshall Scull, *Hunting in the Arctic and Alaska* (1914).

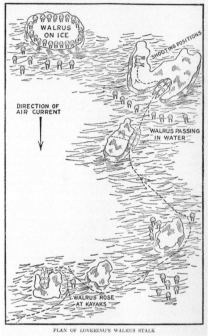

continued, carried on by small-scale sealers, traders and specialist walrus hunters, mainly from Norwegian vessels. As walruses became scarce, hunters were forced to go further afield, and became unwelcome visitors. In 1911 the Danish government sent warships to Greenland to arrest American walrus hunters, and in the same year Russia sought to enact legislation to protect the fisheries of the White Sea, where according to the London *Times*, 'Norwegian poachers are said to be responsible for the wholesale extermination of walrus and seal.'[29]

The belated protection of walrus herds appeared as a response to human rather than walrus needs. Indigenous people found their traditional lifestyles, and even survival, threatened. European and American walrus hunters lost their livelihood. Useful commodities became scarce. In all cases, however, protection measures were introduced after commercial hunting had become unprofitable, due to scarcity or lack of demand. While money remained to be made, hunting continued, even when hunters and governments alike believed that the species was doomed. As one commentator wrote in 1903, the walrus's

> days are numbered because neither the British Government, nor the Russian, nor the Danish, nor that of the United States, as Governments, care one particle about zoology, or the saving from extinction of remarkable mammals which can be slaughtered for 'sport' or commerce.[30]

Walrus protection legislation passed between the 1900s and 1950s largely restricted hunting to indigenous peoples, to the dismay of some communities that depended on the cash input provided by big-game hunters. In Alaska, a ban on non-indigenous hunting in 1909 had a detrimental effect on the walrus population, as the indigenous inhabitants deprived of income from guiding big-game hunters took more walruses for their ivory, forcing a ban on hunting solely for ivory in 1915. Baffin Bay and the Davis Strait were heavily hunted in the 1920s, as walrus hides had again increased in value due to their use as the inner tubes of car tyres. Non-indigenous walrus hunting in Canadian waters was banned in 1931, and protests at large Norwegian kills of over 2,000 walruses in this area between 1949 and 1951 led to a ban by Norway on any hunting of walruses by its citizens anywhere. The banning of walrus hunting in Arctic nations did not benefit walruses that strayed outside their normal range, however. In 1959 it was reported that the Japanese airforce was pursuing a 'war on walruses', which were said to be damaging fishing nets around the island of Todo-Iwa. Shotgun fire did not drive the walruses away, so they were machine-gunned from jet fighters.[31]

The last nation to commercially hunt walruses was the Soviet Union. After the Revolution of 1917, the USSR did not initially take much interest in its Arctic possessions, but in the 1930s a campaign began to develop the region. Stalin had spent some time as an exile in the Siberian Arctic prior to 1917, and the triumph of Soviet man over the harsh Arctic environment became a prominent theme. Indigenous peoples were absorbed into the new system. Native hunting was subsidized, and in the 1920s state walrus-hunting vessels were introduced. Thousands of walruses were killed each year until declining numbers led to protective measures in 1956. The Pacific walrus migrates between Russian and American waters; both Soviet and American marine mammalogists were aware of the problems, but not much could be done without cooperation. Although the Cold War was then at its height, scientists began to work together in the late 1950s, eventually becoming part of the pioneering U.S.–USSR Environmental Protection Agreement of 1972. The American walrus biologist Francis H. Fay, an early member of this programme, even learned Russian in order to be able to translate the papers of his Soviet colleagues. Pacific walrus populations subsequently made a good recovery from overhunting, possibly because vast areas of molluscs had been left undisturbed for so many years that large additional food sources were available. Like the Atlantic walrus, however, their range has been restricted by hunting: in the past Pacific walruses were found in the much more southerly regions of Kamchatka and the Sea of Okhotsk, to which they have never returned.

The history of the walrus in the heyday of empire and industry is undoubtedly a sorry tale. In pursuing their manifest destinies, colonial powers had no concern for sustainability or animal life.

Indeed, animal populations seemed so vast that their eradication appeared inconceivable. Unlike indigenous peoples, colonists saw themselves as an entirely different category of being from animals with 'dominion over the fish of the sea . . . and over every creeping thing that creepeth upon the earth', as the Bible puts it (Genesis 1:26). Animals were regarded as a resource no different from coal or soybeans; the language of hunting is one of commodities rather than of living beings. Sea mammals are 'harvested' like crops, although they were not planted, and taken from 'fisheries', although they are not fish. Sport hunters do not hunt walruses, but 'walrus', a commodified noun rather than a series of individuals; animals are not 'killed', but 'taken', 'bagged' or

Skinning walruses on board the Dundee whaler *Maud,* 20th century.

'lost'. Nowadays, hunting sea mammals for fun, profit or scientific reasons is largely condemned as cruel and unnecessary. Commercial walrus hunting was banned by the time environmental awareness rose to prominence in the 1960s, so the walrus has never been the focus of a popular conservation campaign as have whales and seals. However, climate change may change that, and, like the whale, the walrus may go from being a distant freakish creature to an icon of a vanishing world. Indeed, for all the ongoing violence that characterizes the history of man's relations with walruses, from commercial hunting in the nineteenth century to the subtler violence of global warming, the walrus has also appeared as a much-loved creature in popular culture: a cuddly figure of fun that has evolved a long way from the hideous sea monster of the past.

4 Walruses in Popular and Visual Culture

On his epic and ultimately unsuccessful journey to reach the North Pole in 1893–6, Fridtjof Nansen encountered a great many walruses. His poignant description of one walrus's death strikingly illustrates the two most recurrent (and seemingly incompatible) modes of representing walruses in the South. On the one hand, the walrus is the demonic brute, fit for nothing but the hunter's rifle. On the other, there is something immediately affecting about the animal's face, its hint of humanity inviting compassion instead of violence:

> In spite of its huge body and shapeless appearance, which called up to the imagination bogie, giant, and kraken, and other evil things, there was something so gently supplicating and helpless in its round eyes as it lay there, that its goblin exterior and one's own need were forgotten in pity for it. It almost seemed like murder. I put an end to its sufferings by a bullet behind the ear, but those eyes haunt me yet; it seemed as if in them lay the prayer for existence of the whole helpless walrus race. But it is lost; it has man as its pursuer.[1]

For all its 'goblin exterior', Nansen cannot help but be haunted by its helpless round eyes as he reflects sorrowfully on the future of the apparently doomed 'walrus race' in the very instant he finishes the animal with a bullet behind the ear. At once a bogie and a vulnerable soul, the walrus of the popular imagination is perhaps above all a complicated creature.

At the end of the nineteenth century, Nansen is writing at what might be thought of as an historical cusp in the representation of the walrus. For centuries, the walrus was seen as a terrifying monster bestriding myth and reality, looming mysteriously out of the uncanny icy domain of the North. As the image of the walrus came to be more familiar outside the Arctic through the eighteenth and nineteenth century's colonial incursions, another tradition develops in which the walrus's unique facial characteristics make it seem a friendly and unintimidating beast. By the late twentieth and early twenty-first centuries, the walrus had come to be something approaching a staple of children's literature, film and TV: generally the most affable of animals, with one or two sinister exceptions. While the walrus's monstrosity expresses its remoteness from the human, the tendency to dress it up with cutesy clothes and comedy voice humanizes it. Although this may seem an improvement from its earlier demonization, the comic walrus is not without its own ethical problems. There is a danger

Bogie, giant, and kraken', Fridtjof Nansen's walrus in *Farthest North* (1893), pastel sketch.

that in seeing the walrus as a caricature we may forget to look at it in its own terms: as an autonomous being apart from, if still interlinked with, our own world. The story of the walrus in popular and visual culture from monster to cartoon is in many ways a tale of the walrus's shadow in the human imagination. Inevitably the way that human ideas and images become attached to animals, even at times subsuming them, influences how we conduct ourselves, collectively, towards them.

Nansen's depiction of the walrus as the 'bogie, giant, and kraken' takes us back to the time at which the Arctic was seen as the end of the world, a demonic realm infested with monsters. The North was a place, as Milton expressed it in *Paradise Lost*, where 'Nature breeds/ Perverse, all monstrous, all prodigious things,/ Abominable, unutterable and worse/ Than fables yet have feigned,

Dangerous monsters: sailors fighting with walruses, engraving by Himeli, *Le Magasin Pittoresque* (1843).

or fear conceived' (Book II, ll. 624–8). The diabolic Arctic has a long history. In the Book of Isaiah, Lucifer plans to set up his throne in the North; in pagan Norse legends the way to Hell lies north-wards.[2] The depredations of the Vikings only encouraged this view. When the monastery of Lindisfarne was savagely attacked in AD 793, the English scholar Alcuin was moved to quote the prophecy of Jeremiah: 'Out of the north an evil shall break forth upon all the inhabitants of the land.'[3] The walrus, then, inhabited the most unpromising of environments.

In medieval Europe, the borders between this world and the next, the real and the supernatural, were more ambiguous than we think of them today. Monsters were widespread. Forests were full of them, and the sea was particularly cursed as the home of the biblical Leviathan or 'the dragon that is in the sea' (Isaiah 27:1). The *Liber monstrorum*, an early English work, describes 120 dif-ferent 'horrible forms of unknown beasts', but does not even start on sea monsters, as:

> Concerning these things I have thought nothing worth writing to you, because they are both innumerable, and knowledge of them is far removed from humankind, as if by the terrifying battlements of the sea-waves, and by a wall of sea.[4]

The large, unfamiliar animals of the North evidently provided some factual basis for these myths. Monsters often appear with walrus-like characteristics, just as walruses were often represented with monstrous ones. A medieval *History of Norway* describes northern seas containing numerous possibly morsine monsters, including 'one-eyed horse-whales with spreading manes', the 'most ferocious beasts ploughing the depths of the sea'.[5] Similarly, *The King's Mirror*, a thirteenth-century Old Norse educational text, identified and accurately described walruses, while also warning of 'voracious and malicious' horse-whales that 'never grow tired of slaying men'.[6]

Among the most notable later sources in reconstructing the ongoing history of the walrus as monster are the decorative maps of the sixteenth and seventeenth centuries. Following the example of Olaus Magnus, a Swedish theologian who wrote an influential *History of the Northern Peoples*, cartographers illustrated seas full of monsters. Olaus's depiction of the walrus of 1539 places the tusks in the lower jaw pointing skywards and features a curious mane of vibrissae (in fact more like spines) at the back of the head, with the walrus pictured clinging on to a cliff face on lizard-like legs. In 1603 the Flemish cartographer Abraham Ortelius produced a striking map of Iceland (a country abounding with sea monsters and today home to the world's only Sea Monster Museum) that pictures the shore surrounded with all manner of menacing brutes, often pictured with gaping mouths and

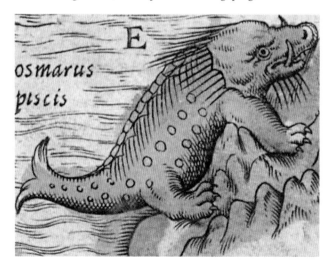

Detail of a walrus from Olaus Magnus's *Carta Marina,* 16th century.

113

prominent teeth, so prominent in fact that stories of the walrus's tusks seem to have infiltrated into the representations of other creatures. Among Ortelius's cast of sea monsters, a walrus is clearly visible, this time with tusks pointing in the right direction, although again with four odd, stumpy legs. Ortelius's source is likely to have been Conrad Gessner, who produced an earlier version of the spiny, cliff-hanging walrus, along with an image that more closely resembles the walrus we would recognize now, at least in the representation of the head, if not the body. Gessner's source in turn was rather an unlikely one. It seems that some-time around 1520 the Norwegian Bishop Erik Valkendorf of Trondheim had sent a walrus head preserved in salt to Pope Leo x. En route to Rome, the head was briefly displayed at the town hall in Strasbourg described as *cetus dentatus* (or toothed whale). There, some curious soul sketched the animal on a wall, filling in the missing details from their imagination. The result, copied by

Walrus from
Abraham Ortelius's
map of Iceland,
*Theatrum Orbis
Terrarum*, 1598.

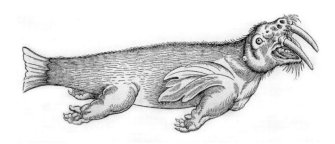

Gessner, has a strange 'wing' above the forelegs (also reproduced in Ortelius's version) and a tail that evokes a fish more than a pinniped, but with a recognizable face at least.[7] Gessner also copies the rhyme written next to the picture by an anonymous graffiti artist that rather poignantly looks at things from the walrus's perspective. 'The Bishop of Trondheim had me stabbed on the shore and sent my head to Pope Leo in Rome, so that many people might see me', the walrus sadly reports.[8]

Other cartographers represented the walrus as remarkably akin to the elephant, quite possibly revealing the ongoing legacy of the mammoth (at this time already extinct for around 4,000 years) in imaginings of the North. Alternatively, this could have been a more pragmatic representation: since it was known that ivory came from elephants, and ivory also came from the North, there must, therefore, be elephants in the North. Martin Waldeseemüller's map of the world of 1516 describes the morsus 'as an elephant-sized animal with two long quadrangular teeth'.[9] The illustration is an almost precise reproduction of the elephant minus the trunk, and with tusks again pointing up rather than down. A later edition of the same map produced by Laurent Fries in 1522 poses another elephantine 'morsus' on the coast of Greenland, this time even going so far as to add in the trunk. John J. McKay, a scholar of mammoths, suggests the possibility that

A 'morsus', something between an elephant and a walrus. Martin Waldseemüller *Carta Marina*, 1516.

the illustrator for these maps was none other than the great German artist Albrecht Dürer.[10] Among Dürer's representations of animals, the most famous is probably his woodcut of a rhinoceros of 1515 with its remarkable sheets of armour, but in an album of 1521 containing 167 drawings of quadrupeds he also included a walrus. Although there is some debate over the translation of the caption that accompanies the picture, the British Museum offers the following: 'That stupid animal of which I have portrayed the head was caught in the Netherlands sea and was twelve brabant ells long with four feet.'[11] With the archaic measurement 'twelve brabant ells' corresponding to about 12 m, there is evidently a degree of the fabulous to Dürer's supersized walrus, but, although rather furrier than might be expected, a walrus it undoubtedly is. Interestingly, Dürer was to reuse the walrus drawing again in 1522, this time in a study for a depiction of a *Virgin and Child with Eight Saints* in which the walrus head becomes the head of a dragon.

The versatility of Dürer's walrus encapsulates its existence on the margins of the real. As well as the confusion between tusks and unicorn horns, walruses have also been identified with a wide variety of mythical creatures, including the much fabled mermaid and the lesser known sea monk. This latter creature was found off the coast of Sweden in 1546 and won its name for its startling familiarity. As two eighteenth-century authorities explained, the animal had 'a human head and face, resembling in appearance the men with shorn heads, whom we call monks'. Looking below the head, the resemblance had its limits: 'the appearance of its lower parts, bearing a coating of scales, barely indicated the torn and severed limbs and joints of the human body'. Fearing such a

Lorentz Fries's revision of Waldseemüller's 'morsus', 1522.

strange being should provide 'a fertile subject for offensive talk', on the king's order 'this abominable creature was immediately buried in the ground'.[12] Although sixteenth-century illustrations give little grounds for thinking that the sea monk was a wandering walrus (or indeed for identifying the sea monk with any creature known today), some scholars have found the walrus to be perhaps the most likely of explanations for this odd find, at least in the baldness of its head and the often cited humanity of its face. And it was the familiar physiognomy of the walrus that also led to its frequent association with mermaids. As the Arctic explorer William Scoresby commented, since the walrus 'is in the habit of rearing its head above water, to look at ships, and other passing objects, it is not at all improbable but that it may have afforded foundation for some of the stories of Mermaids'.[13] Similarly, the Scottish myth of the selkie, an animal that moved between human and seal form, may owe something to the walrus. Even the Loch Ness monster, that most famous of all mysterious creatures, was suggested in 2000 by a team of Swedish researchers

Albrecht Dürer,
Walrus, from his
*Tagebuch der Reise
in die Niederlande*,
1521, pen and
brown ink with
watercolour.

to be a subspecies of the walrus, based on unidentified sound recordings from the loch which are only matched in frequency by the vocalizations of walruses, elephant seals and killer whales.

One explanation for the walrus's apparent metamorphosis into an array of weird and wonderful animals in the eyes of visitors to the North is the distorting optical effect of Arctic light. In the late nineteenth century, for example, the Finnish Baron Nils Adolf Erik Nordenskiöld described his uncertainty in identifying a 'dark border' that was seen 'through the mist at the horizon':

Charles Heath, engraving in George Shaw, *General Zoology* (1800), based on a drawing from Hessel Gerritsz, *Histoire du Pays Nomme Spitsberghe* (1613).

It was taken for the island which we were bound for, and it was not at first considered remarkable that the dark border rose rapidly, for we thought that the mist was dispersing and in consequence of that more of the land was visible. Soon two white snow-fields, that we had not observed before, were seen on both sides of the land, and immediately after this was changed to a sea-monster, resembling a walrus-head, as large as a mountain. This got life and motion, and finally sank all at once to the head of a common walrus, which lay on a piece of ice in the neighbourhood of the boat; the white tusks formed the snow-fields and the dark-brown round head the mountain.[14]

The monstrosity that shadowed the walrus's presence in the human mind for centuries may, in part, be a mirage through which it became magnified into a form even more extraordinary than its own striking appearance.

The seventeenth century saw a marked decline in the representation of sea monsters on maps as fantastic creations and their replacement with more accurate illustrations of known creatures.

In 1594 a real 'wall-rusch' killed during the Arctic voyage of Willem Barentsz was brought to Amsterdam. The subsequent account of the journey contained the first picture of a walrus in the South drawn from life.[15] Images of walruses come progressively to more closely resemble the animal we know today. A significant later staging post in the development of representations of the walrus was the work of the French naturalist Georges-Louis Leclerc, Comte de Buffon, author of the magisterial 36-volume *Histoire Naturelle, générale et particulière*, published between 1749 and 1788. Buffon's account of the 'walrus, morse or sea-cow' is lengthy and detailed, or, as he puts it, 'a tolerable complete history of this animal' with a sober, scholarly tone and no room for talk of fabulous beings.[16] Even in the mid-eighteenth century, Buffon is able to remark on the significant reduction in the walrus's range, 'the whale fishery having disturbed and driven them away'.[17] While illustrations to some editions of Buffon's *Histoire* reveal an animal significantly slimmer than the walrus we recognize, the English edition of 1792 reveals a satisfyingly plump creature. The stubby legs of the

Illustration from Comte de Buffon, *Histoire Naturelle*, trans. William Smellie (1785).

Renaissance are replaced by the characteristic pinniped flippers, the trunk is gone and the tusks point down.

The taxonomic developments of the eighteenth and nineteenth centuries, then, saw the scientific walrus gradually become established. This did not mean, however, that the walrus as sea monster was consigned to the dustbin of history. As Nansen's remarks from the 1890s demonstrate, it would be a long time before the walrus would entirely shed its demonic image in accounts of Arctic exploration: reality and myth continued to be intertwined. The idea of the walrus as a 'devil incarnate', in the words of Charles F. Hall's mid-nineteenth-century description, was just too enticing an image to lay aside, and one that was nourished by the rise of the Gothic as a significant literary genre.[18] Mary Shelley's *Frankenstein* (1818) placed the monster firmly back in the Arctic, her famous creature escaping from Dr Frankenstein through 'immense and rugged mountains of ice'.[19] Moreover, the renewal of British efforts to find the Northwest Passage, beginning in 1818 and climaxing with the search for, and ultimate grisly discovery of, the Franklin expedition, sparked a period of tremendous popular interest in the Arctic that routinely returned to the theme of the sublime and awful North. Explorers' journals were bestsellers, and Arctic panoramas, giant moving paintings that were early precursors of the cinema, left visitors pleasantly terrified. Such was the vogue for the North that the Arctic turned up in the most incongruous places. Edward Bulwer Lytton's poem *King Arthur* (1848) sends the titular monarch and his knights off on a Viking voyage, where they are attacked by 'shapeless, grisly swarms' of monstrous walruses.[20]

One distinct literary form that seemed particularly keen to continue to provide a habitat for the diabolic walrus was the boy's-own adventure. These texts often drew extensively on published non-fiction, particularly where they could borrow sensational, strange or violent material from an original account of a journey

Arctic sublime: Franklin's ships *Erebus* and *Terror* with walruses in the foreground. Illustration from Francis Watt, ed., *Pictorial Chronicles of the Mighty Deep* (1887).

to a remote corner of the world. Such writing was exceptionally popular and closely involved with the imperialist ideology of Victorian Britain, generally based around a youthful hero's all-conquering sojourn in Africa or India in the service of the Crown. Today, with its unapologetic racism and at times extraordinarily gory depictions of big-game hunting, boy's-own fiction makes for disturbing reading. One author in particular who took this genre into the Arctic was the prolific Scotsman R. M. Ballantyne, most famous for the children's classic *The Coral Island* (1857). Ballantyne had worked as a clerk for the Hudson's Bay Company in northern Canada as a young man. As his literary career developed, he returned to the North time and again as the setting for his mostly rather formulaic narratives. Given the genre's taste for the weird and spectacular, it is hardly surprising that walruses should be not infrequent visitors to the pages of these Northern adventures.

Ballantyne's first Arctic adventure is *Ungava: A Tale of Esquimau Land* (1858), a novel which makes the most of the walrus's reputed grotesquery in an account of an Inuit hunting trip. Predictably for Ballantyne, the walrus

> was truly a savage-looking monster, as large as a small elephant, and having two tusks of a foot and a half long. The face bore a horrible resemblance to that of a man. Its crown was round and bulging, its face broad and massive, and a thick, bristling moustache – rough as the spines of a porcupine – covered its upper lip, and depended in a shaggy dripping mass over its mouth.

Ballantyne never himself encountered a walrus in the flesh, so his depiction is merely a recycling of the familiar tropes of other accounts. Rather than finding the walrus's resemblance to man moving, Ballantyne is horrified by the parody of humanity he imagines in its bulging eyes and bristling moustache. In characteristic adventure fiction mode, the discovery of a large, odd-looking creature means that its demise must be just around the corner. Although the walrus in its flight from the indigenous hunter Annatock seems momentarily to be 'actually endued with reason', Ballantyne is unrestrained in his depiction of its death: 'Harpoon after harpoon was driven into the walrus; again and again the lance pierced deep into its side and drank its life-blood.' In what is a familiar pattern in this kind of writing, Ballantyne's walrus bizarrely appears to crave its own death, 'grinning and bellowing as if in disappointment' during a lull in the assault. The walrus, of course gets exactly what Ballantyne thinks it wants; the hunt resumes, the 'unearthly-looking monster smashing the ice around it, and lashing the blood-stained sea into foam'.[21] In a period in which the economic value of the walrus was beginning to be firmly established, the animal's death wish appears convenient, to say the least. Later, in his penultimate novel *The Walrus Hunters* (1893), Ballantyne would return to walruses at even greater length. The intervening decades between *Ungava* and this novel had seen Ballantyne lose none of his gruesome enthusiasm for hunting scenes. The later text, indeed, saw him especially fascinated by the penetration of the walrus's body: a shot at one of a walrus's 'glaring eyes' leaves it with a 'bullet in the brain', while an old bull is repulsed by a hunter sending about two feet of 'paddle down its throat'.[22]

Monstrosity, therefore, invited cruelty. Another notable author in the adventure tradition provided a more oblique reference to the common perception of the walrus as a fierce, wicked being. In his celebrated pirate story *Treasure Island* (1883), Robert Louis Stevenson, on whom Ballantyne was a significant influence, named the vessel of the villainous Captain Flint the *Walrus*. Ships were commonly named after sea creatures at this time, but Stevenson's

choice is telling. Like pirates, walruses were bad eggs, inhabiting
the margins of the geographical world just as pirates dwelled at
the margins of society. But the nineteenth century's most high-
profile popular cultural walrus was perhaps rather more complex
than the straightforwardly demonized beasts of Ballantyne's

A homesick walrus enjoying an ice-cream with his Arctic friends in a French cafe, Jean-Ignace-Isidore Grandville, *Scènes de la Vie Privée et Publique des Animaux*, 1842.

imagination. Lewis Carroll's *Through the Looking-Glass* (1872), the sequel to *Alice's Adventures in Wonderland* (1865), embraces the peculiar, so it is hardly surprising that a walrus should appear among Carroll's surreal cast of talking animals. 'The Walrus and the Carpenter' is a poem narrated to Alice by Tweedledee with the encouragement of his brother Tweedledum. The poem is conceived, of course, as nonsense, part of a nineteenth-century genre of verse of which Edward Lear was the other most notable exponent. Lear, indeed, offered some walruses of his own, writing mysteriously of a 'pea green gamut on a distant plain/ Where wily walruses in congress meet'.[23] Sir John Tenniel's original illustrations to *Through the Looking-Glass* may justly be thought to comprise the birth of the cartoon walrus. Tenniel has the Walrus neatly attired in bow-tie, waistcoat, shirt, jacket and baggy trousers, standing upright on comically splayed feet. Later illustrators added other flourishes. Peter Newell puts the Walrus into a Victorian bathing suit, while Mervyn Peake (author of the *Gormenghast* trilogy) gives him a cane and cigar, clutched between unmistakeably human fingers. All in all, the Walrus looks kindly enough, but for all its cuddly appearance, it has a mean streak.

Carroll's poem, in short, unfolds like this. The Walrus and his Carpenter companion stroll along a beach, upset initially by the quantities of sand which even seven maids with seven mops sweeping for half a year would fail to clean up, in the Carpenter's tearful opinion. It is the relationship of the two main characters with a group of oysters, however, that provides the nub of the poem. At first, the Walrus beseeches the oysters to join them in

Sir John Tenniel, *The Walrus and the Carpenter*, illustration from Lewis Carroll, *Through the Looking-Glass* (1872).

Peter Newell, 'The eldest Oyster winked his eye, And shook his heavy head', *Through the Looking-Glass* (1902).

a 'pleasant walk . . . along the briny beach'. Although the eldest oyster is having none of it, four younger oysters follow the walrus's call and are quickly followed by 'more, and more, and more'. Then, resting on a rock, the Walrus makes his famous announcement:

> 'The time has come,' the Walrus said,
>   'To talk of many things:
> Of shoes – and ships – and sealing-wax –
>   Of cabbages – and kings'.

Alas, the walrus has more than a story in mind for the oysters. Calling for a loaf, pepper and vinegar, the Walrus ignores the molluscs' complaints and he and the Carpenter begin to eat them. The Walrus at least shows a certain regret ('"It seems a shame," the Walrus said,/ "To play them such a trick"'), but continues to devour them through his moral discomfort, sorting out those 'of largest size' with 'sobs and tears'. The Walrus's companion, however, is relatively unmoved: '"O Oysters," said the Carpenter,

"You've had a pleasant run"'. At the poem's conclusion, Alice announces that she prefers the Walrus to the Carpenter because he at least was 'a *little* sorry for the oysters', although she revises her opinion when Tweedledee points out that he ate more than the Carpenter despite his apparent sensitivity. Alice finally concedes they 'were *both* very unpleasant characters'.[24]

Assigning meaning to nonsense is always a risky business, although this has done nothing to prevent a giddying array of interpretations of the poem from emerging, varying from the plausible to the eccentric. Indeed, the story of the poem's composition emphasizes the difficulty of interpreting the text too literally. It was in fact Tenniel who decided on the identity of the Carpenter, having been given a choice by Carroll of carpenter, butterfly or baronet; it was the scansion that mattered to Carroll rather than any particular significance attached to woodwork. (And why he chose a walrus is unclear; the walrus in Sunderland Museum has been claimed as his inspiration, but it was acquired too late. Another intriguing suggestion is that Carroll's clergyman brother-in-law kept a stuffed walrus in his rectory.[25]) This back story seems to put paid to some religious readings that take the Carpenter's profession as a cue to interpret him as Christ. The Walrus in this view becomes either the Buddha, because of his girth, or the Hindu elephant god Ganesha, because of the tusks. With the oysters lured away from their natural state only to be preyed upon by these plausible intruders, the poem as a whole then becomes an impassioned plea against organized religion which sits uncomfortably with what we know of Carroll, who was a deeply religious man and the Deacon of Christ Church, Oxford. Sexualized readings have also been suggested, fuelled by unsubstantiated rumours that Charles Lutwidge Dodgson, the man behind the pen-name Lewis Carroll, may have had an inappropriate relationship with Alice Liddell, the girl behind the fictional Alice. Consequently, the Walrus and Carpenter become sexual predators and the oysters their young victims in what would then seem a concealed (and rather peculiar) confession of sexual misconduct. Carroll's initial plan to have the Walrus and Carpenter hand-in-hand has also provoked the suggestion of a homosexual sub-text, the oysters (a word blending 'boys', 'choristers' and 'ostlers', according to one commentator) representing abused schoolboys.[26]

If explicitly theological or erotic readings seem to go too far, there appears nonetheless to be a clear moral agenda in the story (although if you take it literally, the only real moral is 'beware of strangers at the seaside').[27] The Walrus after all realizes the consequences of his actions without giving any thought to acting differently, weeping for the oysters as he gobbles them up. Suggestions that the poem may express an early form

A slimmed-down, dog-like walrus, *Dictionnaire Pittoresque d'Histoire Naturelle et des Phénomènes* (1833–40).

of environmentalism are somewhat more credible. In a letter to *The Spectator* of 1875, Carroll ironically noted how the 'torture of the animal world' had become one of the 'steps of the ladder by which man is ascending to his higher civilization'.[28] The Walrus's simultaneous destruction of and lament for the oysters may therefore suggest an all-too familiar human approach to the environment: for all our appreciation of the natural world, we can't stop consuming it. Consequently, the oysters would correspond to the planet and their predators would represent different shadings of human folly, with the tender-hearted walrus and the hard-hearted carpenter both working towards the same dismal outcome. The early part of the poem does feature an eerie ecological atmosphere ('No birds were flying overhead – / There were no birds to fly') that might lend some support to an environmentalist approach.

Other political readings have looked beyond the poem's nineteenth-century context to identify it with later historical developments. Stalin, and assorted other dictators, have been suggested as historical figures evoked by Carroll's characters. As J. B. Priestley puts it, in 'The Walrus and the Carpenter' we are 'brought face to face with the eternal figures of political leadership'.[29] The novelist Henry Kingsley, brother of the more famous Charles and friend of Carroll, has one of his characters read the poem as an allegory for the Franco–Prussian War. Here, the Walrus is the 'Emperor of Germany' and the Carpenter is 'the Archduke Charles'.[30] The Walrus's political credentials were revisited in the 1970s when the former Prime Minister Harold Macmillan appeared in the role in a cartoon by Ralph Steadman in *The Times* that accompanies a scathing article by Bernard Levin on the decolonization of Africa. With his trademark moustache and hangdog expression, Macmillan makes rather a good walrus, but the symbolism was not gauged to be complimentary;

nor indeed was the casting of Harold Wilson as the Carpenter. For Levin, presiding over the break-up of the British Empire made Macmillan and Wilson into exactly the kind of dissemblers Carroll portrayed.

Just under 100 years after the publication of *Through the Looking-Glass*, Carroll's poem provided the stimulus for another much-analysed walrus. John Lennon was reportedly dismayed to discover after having written 'I am the Walrus' how far the walrus's apparent politics diverged from his own. While Lennon was the hippy peace activist, the walrus was the tyrant. 'I am the Walrus' would seem, then, to be a terrible mistake. Some Lennon scholars, however, claim to have located a profound and serious

Ralph Steadman, Harold Macmillan and Harold Wilson as the Walrus and the Carpenter, illustration from *The Times*, 1970.

engagement with Carroll's work in The Beatles' song that rules out such an oversight. Lennon was undoubtedly deeply influenced by Carroll, finding his interest in the absurd and the mischievous nourished by the Alice stories. Significantly, it is not just the walrus that makes the journey from Alice to 'I am the Walrus'. Humpty Dumpty, who appears shortly after the Walrus in *Through the Looking-Glass*, is translated by Lennon into 'the eggman'. Like Tweedledee, Humpty Dumpty also offers Alice a poem, this time one in which fish rather than oysters are earmarked for a meal. The fish, it seems, bring this fate on themselves by refusing to obey an unspecified request by Humpty Dumpty, a decision which has some menacing consequences. 'My heart went hop, my heart went thump:/ I filled the kettle at the pump', Humpty Dumpty ominously explains as he reflects on the fate of the fish. But while the oysters are consumed one and all by the Walrus and Carpenter, Humpty Dumpty goes hungry as the fish remain behind a locked door. For Michael E. Roos, the connection between Humpty Dumpty and the Walrus is the key to the meaning of Lennon's song. Both characters use language to lure their victims (or potential victims) to a grisly end. The song, therefore, becomes a condemnation of a widespread culture of deception, or as Roos puts it: 'We are all con men . . . and the implication is that the con game makes the world go around.'[31] Just like the eggman Humpty Dumpty, the world is hollow; Lennon is the walrus because he too participates in this empty, exploitative world. The Beatles' legions of fans, to Roos, are mere oysters swept along 'toward a dream he no longer believed in'.[32]

Later Lennon would claim in 'Glass Onion', that it was Paul McCartney who was in fact the Walrus. This has been interpreted both as an act of reconciliation from Lennon to McCartney in a period of antagonism between the two great songwriters (that is, if you think being a walrus is generally a good thing). Alternatively, the line has been read as a kind of two fingers to McCartney: it was McCartney, Lennon suggests, who was the duplicitous one. When The Beatles had come to dress up in trippy outfits for the cover of *Magical Mystery Tour*, the album containing 'I am the Walrus', Paul was indeed the Walrus, complete with tusks and flippers and a rather sinister black woolly jumper (a costume which incidentally has been used as evidence to support a long-standing conspiracy theory in which McCartney was said to have died in the late 1960s, to be replaced by a weirdly identical double). Roos's argument about 'I am the Walrus' is detailed and convincing, although he is not able to explain away all the bizarre images of Lennon's song ('semolina pilchards' and 'elementary penguins' are a bridge too far, for example). Intriguingly, Lennon returned again to the walrus in his first solo album in 1970, declaiming that he was no longer the Walrus, but by then simply John, as if he had moved beyond the glib culture of stardom associated with The Beatles (if that is what the initial reference signified) towards something approaching self-acceptance. In the end, both Carroll's and Lennon's walruses will always leave us with more questions than answers. Mind-altering drugs have been implicated in the creation of both 'The Walrus and the Carpenter' and 'I am the Walrus': opium in Carroll's case, LSD in Lennon's. What may appear now to be full of teasingly hidden meanings may in fact mean nothing. Carroll was adamant that his poem really *was* nonsense. Lennon reportedly wanted to mess with the heads of a bourgeois intellectual community who sought to read too much into his writing. Sometimes, to adapt a phrase of Freud's, a walrus is just a walrus.

What Lewis Carroll's poem and Lennon's song do perhaps reveal, however, is how seductive the figure of the walrus became in the era of mass-produced popular culture beginning in the nineteenth century, an effect that is especially apparent in the walrus's long career in advertising (might Carroll's Walrus be a venture capitalist luring all us gullible oysters into the banking crisis?). While nineteenth-century economic developments made use of the body of the walrus, corporations in the twentieth and twenty-first centuries have made repeated use of its image. Many walrus-based advertisements have responded directly to Carroll. The takeover of the Callard & Bowser confectionery company by Guinness in the 1950s, for instance, was announced by a walrus, evidently closely based on Tenniel's illustration, standing above Alice and the carpenter carrying a pair of trays, one holding a pint of Guinness, the other a box of Callard & Bowser butterscotch. The walrus's most famous lines are adjusted accordingly:

> 'The time has come,' the Walrus said,
>   'To say a thing or two:
> Of hops – and crops – and butterscotch –
>   And what is Good for You

Amand von Schweiger-Lerchenfeld, *Von Ocean zu Ocean; Eine Schilderung des Weltmeeres und seines Lebens* (1885).

ARCTIC SPORT.

These sportsmen hunting in the Artic Cold
Declare the "Chest-Shield" worth its weight in gold
(Over)

'No more colds!
No more weak
lungs!', U.S.
advertisement
for a 'chest-shield'
patent undershirt,
1882.

And whether toffee's nice to drink –
Or stout is made to chew.'

Carrying on the enthusiasm of drinks companies for walruses, in 1960 the vodka giants Smirnoff revealed a carpenter and a walrus sharing a vodka gimlet above a caption that reads 'Said the Walrus to the Carpenter: Your Gimlet is Sublime'. Although the Smirnoff walrus looms somewhat above his human companion, the advert, as with Guinness a few years before, seems to miss the sinister implications of Carroll's poem. The walrus is the kind of animal you would happily share a drink with.

Even taking into account the phenomenal popular cultural legacy of the Alice stories, the walrus has appeared in an astonishing array of advertisements, most of which have no explicit connection with Carroll. The twenty-first century alone has seen a remarkable proliferation of walrus marketing campaigns. To name but a few, the car companies Volkswagen and Fiat have both been drawn to walruses, with Fiat even appearing to squeeze one behind the wheel. Yamaha announced a new outboard motor with a waldog (with the body of a walrus and the head of a dog,

BERT LAHR IS THE CARPENTER IN THIS SMIRNOFF WONDERLAND

SAID THE WALRUS TO THE CARPENTER: "YOUR GIMLET IS SUBLIME!"

A good Vodka Gimlet tastes limey—but sublimely *dry*. Its clean tang of lime is subtle, a whisper rather than a shout. To give this lordly cocktail true dryness and real gusto, use smooth Smirnoff Vodka . . . and genuine, imported Rose's Lime Juice. One thing more. Stirring keeps a Gimlet *cloudless*. So shake your head if you see it shaken—or stirred with anything but Smirnoff!

it leaves you breathless

SMIRNOFF® VODKA GIMLET
Add 1 part Rose's Lime Juice to 4 or 5 parts Smirnoff. Stir well and serve over ice in a cocktail or Old Fashioned glass.

$\mathcal{Smirnoff}$
THE GREATEST NAME IN **VODKA**

80 AND 100 PROOF. DISTILLED FROM GRAIN. STE. PIERRE SMIRNOFF FLS. (DIV. OF HEUBLEIN), HARTFORD, CONN.

combining canine fidelity with a walrus's watery prowess). A slump in sales in 2011 prompted the retailer Argos to turn to a walrus (and a couple of penguins) to promote a new delivery service. For the most part such ads trade on a familiar set of ideas: these are fat, friendly creatures with funny faces. The guiding principle seems to be that, despite the menacing undercurrents of Carroll's poem, people like walruses.

But sometimes people like walruses too much. The appearance of a walrus in an ad for Skittles sweets in 2012 produced an outcry resulting in the unforgettable headline in the *Huffington Post*, 'One Million Moms Decries Bestiality Themes in New Walrus Skittles Ad'.[33] The offending 30 seconds opens with an attractive blonde noisily kissing a walrus on a couch. Alas, the happy couple are interrupted by an attractive brunette who believes the walrus to be her boyfriend, Bobby. Not the case, counters attractive blonde: 'this isn't Bobby, he just looks like Bobby'. 'Oh', responds attractive brunette, not entirely convinced. The point (apparently) is that Skittles sweets look like one thing on the outside, but on the inside they are something else. 'Deceive the rainbow' the ad's final

Smirnoff vodka advertisement, 1960s, a pastiche of the Walrus and Carpenter illustrations from Carroll's *Through the Looking-Glass*. Actor Bert Lahr features as the carpenter.

Walrus on a Soviet stamp, c. 1970s.

caption reveals, hence the mistaken boyfriend/walrus plotline. The conservative pressure group One Million Moms was outraged that the manufacturers of such a popular confection should appear to be taking 'lightly the act of bestiality' and demanded that the parent company Wrigley pull the 'disgusting' ad immediately. Wrigley responded by claiming that they 'don't believe this imaginary situation promotes harm or inappropriate behavior with animals'. They are just a 'fun-loving candy brand'. So, reading between the lines, walruses are fun creatures.

Part of One Million Moms' problem with the ad was that it was not the kind of message that any company should be sending to American children. Their dismay may in part be connected to the status of walruses as much-loved animals in children's literature and film since the mid-twentieth century. Wrigley, then, were debasing an icon of children's culture. Just like the marketing walrus, the children's TV walrus has had many incarnations. In 1951 *Alice in Wonderland* got the Disney treatment. Though not in the original book, the Walrus and the Carpenter were too good to miss, and the poem is set to music. Disney's Walrus is a tuskless, blimpish plutocrat who eats all the oysters himself, leaving the working-class carpenter to go hungry. The first instalment of the *Noggin the Nog* series by Oliver Postgate and Peter Firmin features Arup the King of the Walruses, who helpfully tows Noggin's ship to the Land of the Midnight Sun in return for some ship's biscuit. The 1940s and '50s animated character Woody Woodpecker found himself up against the comedy antagonist Wally the Walrus in a number of short films starting with *The Beach Nut* in 1944. Wally is sleepy, gluttonous and speaks in a generic Northern European accent (except in *The Reckless Driver* of 1946, in which he is reconfigured as a New York cop). Less well known, perhaps, but quite similar to Wally, is Chumley the Walrus from *Tennessee Tuxedo and his Tales* of the 1960s. Tennessee is a penguin and Chumley, as the name suggests, is his best friend. While Tennessee is smart and ambitious, Chumley is clumsy and slow-witted. The BBC children's animated series *Octonauts* recently featured a colony of Liverpudlian walruses (evidently playing on the connection with The Beatles), who appear aggressive at first but mellow after the chief walrus has a twisted flipper healed by Peso Penguin.

Some recent cartoons have featured notably less likeable walruses. *The Simpsons Movie* includes the video game Grand Theft Walrus, in which a walrus, complete with bling and a red sports car, guns down a penguin in a drive-by shooting. *Family Guy* went even further in debunking the benevolence of the cartoon walrus with the 'walrus backed Nanookwaffe' in which walruses appear in the cavalry of a kind of Northern Nazis. A sprinkling of other truly menacing examples survive the twentieth century's Disneyfication of the walrus, surely the finest being Ray Harryhausen's 'Walrus Giganticus' from the film *Sinbad and the Eye of the Tiger* (1977). But when a Japanese monster film of 1962 featured a giant walrus terrorizing the North Pole, it was subsequently edited out for the U.S. release, reportedly because the distributors found the addition of a walrus too comical. The monster had been trumped by the cartoon (although the decision could have been made for sound artistic reasons, since, according to one critic, the walrus kills the film stone dead). In literature, few walrus monsters survive. Laurie Foos's novel *Portrait of the Walrus by a Young Artist* of 1997 features a teenage girl obsessed by walruses, possibly as a metaphor for her fear of her own sexuality. The walruses return her interest, pursuing her through Florida, until they stampede on a highway and are euthanized by law enforcement officers.[34] And inevitably demonic walruses appear, leading the fish army, in the Jane Austen mashup *Sense and Sensibility and Sea Monsters*.[35] But these are the exceptions to

Ray Harryhausen's terrifying 'Walrus Giganticus', from Sam Wanamaker (dir.), *Sinbad and Eye of the Tiger* (1977).

the overwhelming trend in the construction of the postmodern walrus, who seems, in contrast to earlier representations, to be a friend to man.

Of course, no sketch of the cultural history of the walrus would be complete without the walrus moustache, the abundant, drooping facial hair most commonly associated with Victorian Britain and a particular sort of colonial, public school type of chap; indeed, the walrus moustache is also referred to as the imperial moustache. Given the remarkable depredations of walrus populations in the nineteenth century, there is a certain irony about the walrus-faced style of the empire builder. The first usage of the term recorded in the *OED* is only from 1918, in the work of the poet Wilfred Owen. By the 1930s the walrus moustache is found attached to Colonel Blimp, David Low's classic cartoon reactionary, who became a byword for unthinking British imperialism. Any list of the great and the good who sported the walrus moustache would be a long one, from Friedrich Nietzsche to Arthur Conan Doyle ('a large man with sad thoughtful eyes and a walrus moustache', as one observer commented), and from *Blackadder Goes Forth*'s General Melchett ('old walrus face' himself) to the Australian fast bowler Merv Hughes. Although recent decades have seen a decline in the popularity of such human vibrissae, the rise of Movember, the moustache-growing charity event, has given walrus whiskers another lease of life, albeit only for one month of the year.

Thinking of this particular style of facial hair in terms of the walrus consolidates the prominence of anthropomorphism in our current representations of walruses. We see this too in the occasional walrus nicknames attached to celebrities. Barry White was the 'walrus of love'; the golfer Craig Stadler is known simply as 'the walrus'. What these two men share is facial hair and a certain rotundity. When a Halloween episode of *The Simpsons* featured a version of H. G. Wells's classic *The Island of Doctor Moreau*, transforming the show's characters into animals, what

A baby Pacific walrus with its walrus moustache.

143

could Homer become but a walrus? Humans, the message seems to unfold, can be like walruses; and walruses, as over 100 years of cartoons have suggested, can be a bit like humans. In parallel to friendly anthropomorphic walruses, performing walruses in zoos and aquaria are trained to present humorous personae, dancing and making funny noises. If audience responses are anything to go by, big, fat, funny-looking things pretending to be people are hilarious, but these are not cartoons: they are real animals living an unnatural life, however well treated they are by their keepers. There is a fine balance to be struck in thinking about the ethics of these representations and in reflecting more broadly on our cultural connections with walruses. Our relationship to walruses should be understood as a complex mixture of kinship and difference. Walruses are both eerily familiar to us – in their care for their young, their gregarious natures and their

A medley of walrus moustaches: (from top, left to right) an old man from Prussia; u.s. Civil War hero General Joshua Chamberlain; Friedrich Nietzsche; Robert Whike, coal miner and great-great grandfather of the authors; Earl Kitchener; u.s. Diplomat Nicholas Fish II; Henry C. Warmoth, Governor of Louisiana; Rudyard Kipling; Robert Peary.

whiskery faces – and utterly alien to us. Walruses are not cutesy cartoons and they are not ours to do with as we please. With the world warming at an alarming rate as a consequence of human industrial cultures, our ethical responsibilities to these strange animals should be pressing.

5 Walruses in a Warming World

In 1869 a Canadian naturalist, J. Bernard Gilpin, read a paper on the walrus to the Nova Scotian Institute of Science. After describing a rare specimen shot near Labrador, he gave an account of the anthropogenic extinction of the southernmost walrus herds, concluding with a string of poignant questions:

> If all created things wage a battle of life, it must be confessed that its tide has turned against these poor sea-horses. Restricted to the high latitudes, deprived of the great enjoyment of basking, lying and resting on the sun-heated sands of latitude 44°N (an enjoyment only comprehended by those who have witnessed it), they are pushed back to the ice floe, to the damp fogs of the arctic circle. The food that fed their progenitors is strange to them. Are their numbers less? Are they of less dimensions? Is their layer of blubber thicker in the greater cold? Are they like their old companion, the great auk destined to become extinct of modern man? Who can answer?[1]

Just as in the late nineteenth century, so today the fate of walruses is hard to know. The IUCN Red List of Threatened Species lists them as 'data deficient'. No one knows for sure how many there are, where they go or if they are increasing or decreasing in number.

The good news is that walruses are now thoroughly protected from the kind of remorseless overhunting that Gilpin was concerned about. Canada banned commercial walrus hunting in 1931; in the U.S. the Congressional Walrus Act of 1941 did the same. Protection measures were also initiated for Svalbard and Greenland in 1952 and in Russia in 1956. In 1960 the Walrus Islands in Alaska's Bristol Bay became a state game sanctuary that at times now hosts up to 14,000 walruses; by the mid-1970s walruses had returned to the Pribilof Islands. Subsistence hunting by indigenous peoples is still permitted but is managed for sustainability. The sale of walrus body parts (most notably ivory) is strictly controlled by the Convention on International Trade in Endangered Species of Wild Fauna and Flora (CITES), which restricts 'international trade in live, animals, parts and derivatives'. The walrus features on CITES' Appendix III, an aspect of the Convention by which specific nations can request international cooperation in regulating the trade in designated animals. Canada listed the walrus on Appendix III in 1975 so that now any purchase of indigenous art carved from walrus tusks needs to be accompanied by a CITES certificate indicating that the animal has been legally hunted. Uncarved walrus ivory cannot now be transported through Canada. In Europe, walruses are a strictly protected species under Appendix II of the Bern Convention on the conservation of European wildlife. They are listed as rare/decreasing in number in the Red Data Book of the Russian Federation and protected by its supporting laws.

Although the development of such legislation during the twentieth century has undoubtedly been a boon to walruses, it has not been without controversy. Significant debates have emerged around the quota system for regulating subsistence hunting by indigenous communities. A large part of the problem is connected to a perceived disconnection between policy makers and the communities that still (after many centuries) derive a large part of their livelihood from hunting marine mammals. In Alaska, the Federal Marine Mammal Act of 1977 saw the federal government set a quota of 3,000 walruses that could be taken annually by indigenous inhabitants. Although the hunt was to be managed by the State of Alaska, repeated petitions to increase the quota in the light of recovering walrus populations fell upon deaf ears and control quickly returned to a federal level. To some, the idea of quotas seemed like a direct attack on a traditional way of life. One hunter complained to legislators that 'You don't know what it is to be an Eskimo. Out here hunting is our way of life. Carving ivory is our livelihood. We don't want welfare supporting us and we don't want to be forced from the villages.'[2] Moreover the very idea of 'subsistence', with its connotations of developmental backwardness and a meagre, hand-to-mouth existence, seemed to reaffirm the racial suppositions of the nineteenth

'Good Hunting. A Walrus Kill. Alaska', early 20th century.

Good Hunting, A Walrus Kill, Alaska.

century. As one Yup'ik man explained, 'Subsistence is more than just hunting and fishing. It's not just physical food – it's spiritual food.'[3] The battle for access to traditional hunting areas becomes a much larger discussion about the fundamental right to practise a cultural and religious identity that has been systematically marginalized since at least the nineteenth century. There is also a related economic argument about the right to continue hunting. Marine mammals provide cheaper and more nutritious foods than the imported goods that in the end perhaps only serve the interests of southern food corporations.

When the walruses of Walrus Islands became formally protected, therefore, this measure was by no means universally popular. The traditional walrus hunt on Round Island (known as Qayassiq in Yup'ik) by people of Togiak became illegal overnight in 1960, although they were not to discover this until 1962, when a small plane belonging to Alaska state law enforcement interrupted a hunt and handcuffed a hunter. It was 1995 before a protracted legal battle to restore the hunt and to prevent what the Togiak Traditional Council called the 'continuing erosion of our culture' came to a resolution.[4] The Alaska Department of Fish and Game (ADFG) and the recently formed Qayassiq Walrus Commission representing the interests of the native villagers would henceforth work with a 'co-management plan' to regulate the walrus hunt. Since 1998 a similar arrangement has existed for other areas of Alaska when a 'Memorandum of Understanding' to jointly administer the indigenous walrus harvest was signed between the ADFG, the U.S. Fish and Wildlife Service and the Eskimo Walrus Commission, an organization which since 1978 has promoted the interests of Alaska's walrus hunting communities. These bodies also work closely with scientists and indigenous walrus hunters across the Bering Strait, supporting hunt monitoring and conservation programmes in Russian Chukotka.

The ongoing importance of walrus hunting in the indigenous North has been consolidated by a cultural renaissance that has seen traditional carving practices become a lucrative commercial enterprise. Sold as souvenirs to travellers since the 1770s, Canadian Inuit artwork was brought to the wider world by the artist James Houston, who became intrigued by art he encountered when visiting Arctic Quebec on a painting trip in the 1940s. Houston subsequently worked to promote the work through the Canadian Handicrafts Guild and after a sell-out exhibition in Montreal in 1949, Inuit art became increasingly sought after. Historically, since the twentieth century, unemployment (along with a range of connected social and health problems) has been a significant issue in native communities. The establishment of arts and craft centres by the Canadian government after the Second World War was identified as one of the main avenues for bringing Inuit into the Canadian cash economy and alleviating poverty. Canada's International and Universal Exposition in 1967, a celebration of Canada's centenary more commonly known as Expo 67, is widely seen as a point at which Inuit art became internationally recognized. Today, works by top Inuit artists such as Kenojuak Ashevak (whose grandfather was reputedly able to transform into a walrus),[5] can fetch thousands of dollars. In 2006 the Toronto auction house Waddington's grossed over $3 million in the sale of Inuit art, including the record sale of $278,500 for an *Umiaq* carving by the northern Quebec artist Joe Talirunili. There are now thriving indigenous artistic communities in Nunavut, Quebec, Labrador and Northwest Territories in Canada as well as in Alaska. Contemporary Inuit artists work in variety of media and styles, and themes are both ancient and modern, but the representation of animals and the natural world, and of shamanic transformations, remain prominent. Notable artistic walruses include the prints and lithographs of the Inupiat Alaskan artist

Ningeokuluk
Teevee, *Imposing
Walrus*, 2009,
drawing featured
on the front
cover of *Inuit
Art Quarterly*,
XXIV/4 (2009).

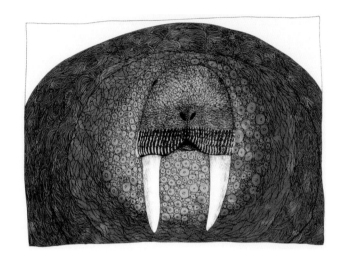

Bernard Tuglamena Katexac such as *Walrus on Migration* (1972) and *Avik* (1963) and the sculptor Peter J. Seeganna's *Wooden Walrus* (1968).

Although carvings are often now made with soapstone, the ancient tradition of using walrus ivory continues, so that the value of walrus ivory is once more at a premium. This economic factor has given rise to a less laudable pursuit known as 'head-hunting', or killing the walrus just for its tusks. In one month in 1981 it was reported that $500,000-worth of uncarved walrus ivory was available on the black market. Although the whole walrus is no longer used by many communities (fewer dogs mean less dog meat is needed), this phenomenon is condemned both by indigenous leaders and state law enforcers. In the 1990s 'Operation Whiteout', an anti-head-hunting investigation carried out by the U.S. Fish and Wildlife Service, resulted in numerous convictions and a raised profile for walrus crime. Pioneering wildlife pathologists performed autopsies on dead walruses in order to determine whether they had been killed illegally: a heroic task considering that, smelly enough when alive, the stench of a long-dead walrus must be unendurable. An education campaign by the Eskimo Walrus Commission, alongside state authorities, has significantly reduced head-hunting.[6]

Another problematic component of the age of subsistence hunting is the re-emergence of walrus hunting for sport. Big-game hunting is big business, despite (or perhaps because of) the decline in many of the target animal populations. The 'Arctic Grand Slam' of caribou, musk ox, polar bear and walrus is an enticing lure to Southern hunters. Since the u.s. Marine Mammal Protection Act of 1972, trophy hunting for walruses in Alaska has been off limits, but in the 1990s Canada permitted a small sport walrus hunt in Nunavut. Expeditions are supervised by Inuit, and the kill forms part of their subsistence quota, but the hunt has attracted argument. This walrus hunting is not the 'wild work' familiar to James Lamont in the nineteenth century; sleeping walruses are shot from close range with high-powered rifles in an experience memorably described by the journalist C. J. Chivers as 'a long

'Arctic Regions', featuring three walruses beneath a looming iceberg, illustration by Adam White from the popular children's natural history, *The Instructive Picture Book* (1867).

boat ride to shoot a very large beanbag chair'.[7] American hunters pay up to $7,000 for the trip, even though u.s. conservation laws prevent them from taking trophies home; the walruses are kept by the Inuit. The philosopher Michael Sandel has discussed the hunt in his book *What Money Can't Buy: The Moral Limits of Markets* (2012). Sandel concludes rather scathingly that

> the desire to kill a helpless mammal at close range, without any challenge or chase, simply to complete a list, is not worthy of being fulfilled, even if doing so provides extra income for the Inuit . . . It's one thing to honor the Inuit way of life and to respect its long-standing reliance on subsistence walrus hunting. It's quite another to convert that privilege into a cash concession in killing on the side.[8]

So, the indigenous hunting of marine mammals remains controversial, surrounded by a host of knotty ethical and political issues. Although walrus hunting is closely monitored to ensure that it remains sustainable, without accurate population figures this is hard to guarantee. Modern technology has made it easier

Illegal walrus products seized by the u.s. Fish and Wildlife Service. Tusks are on the right; the tusk-like objects in the centre are penis bones.

to kill: the replacement of harpoons with guns in indigenous hunting has significantly increased 'struck and lost' rates (in which the walrus is killed but not retrieved). In 1923 over 1,000 walrus carcasses were washed up in Alaska, shot and sunk before the hunters could reach them.[9] Even today, 'struck and lost' rates of up to 40–50 per cent have been estimated, so that in some areas the use of harpoons when hunting at sea has become mandatory. Scientists have suggested that some walrus populations, notably two out of the three Atlantic walrus populations in Greenland, and possibly even the more numerous Pacific walrus, may be over-exploited.[10] In response to these findings, Greenland introduced hunt quotas in 2006. However, disputes have arisen concerning the scientific data on which hunting restrictions are premised. In the 1970s the International Whaling Commission, in response to a report estimating a population possibly only in the hundreds, banned indigenous hunting of the bowhead whale in the Bering Sea. Inupiat subsistence whalers protested, claiming their experience indicated much higher numbers of whales. The Inupiat were proved right, and regained their right to hunt.[11] But ongoing co-management plans between indigenous leaders and government agencies do at least give some grounds for optimism that walruses will not be pushed to the brink of extinction again, by hunting at any rate. The walrus, one might hope, is safe.

But global warming changes everything.

The ice-loving walrus is one of the animals most threatened by climate change. The Arctic is warming at twice the global rate, and the ice is melting. In 2012 summer sea ice shrank to its lowest recorded extent: less than half the area of 40 years ago. Within twenty years the Arctic may be completely free of ice in summer.[12] Walruses use sea ice for a variety of purposes. They rest on the ice while feeding at sea, use it as a safe place to breed and care for young and travel on ice during migration. Pacific walruses,

Polar bears hunting walruses, Chukchi engraving on walrus tusk, 1940s.

particularly females and young, spend more time on sea ice than their Atlantic cousins. In the absence of sea ice, Pacific walruses are forced to resort to terrestrial haul-outs, where they are vulnerable to disturbance.[13] Fear spreads quickly in herd animals, causing terrified walruses to stampede towards the safety of the sea, trampling smaller and weaker animals. Polar bears routinely use walrus panic as a hunting strategy in the hope that in the ensuing chaos an animal might be killed or injured. Walruses have sharp hearing, and unexpected noises generated by human activity, particularly ship or aircraft noise, can cause stampedes. In 2007, when sea ice shrank to a record low, unprecedented numbers of walruses hauled out on the coast of Chukotka with up to 70,000 animals crowded together on the beaches. Observers estimated that stampedes killed between 3,000 and 10,000 walruses, including most of that year's newborns and 1,500 breeding females.[14] Many pregnant females miscarried. Such disturbances also imperil surviving herd members, increasing stress and impeding feeding and suckling of calves. Stampedes can even cause walruses to abandon traditional haul-out areas permanently, further restricting their habitat. The loss of ice threatens young Pacific walruses at sea as well as on land. Atlantic walruses feed near to the coast, but many Pacific walrus feeding grounds are far from land. Without ice to rest on, adult walruses must commute to their feeding grounds from coastal haul-outs, expending more energy and making it more difficult to care for their young.

The Arctic ecosystem is a complex web of interrelationships. Walruses are considered a 'keystone' species, one that has a disproportionately large impact on its ecosystem. Grubbing around on the ocean floor searching for food, walruses release buried nutrients that feed many other animals, a process known as bioturbation. A reduction in the walrus population will mean that less food is available for other organisms. Conversely, walruses themselves depend on other creatures. Climate change will have far-reaching effects, and factors that do not threaten walruses themselves may endanger their prey. One such problem is ocean acidification, which to the marine biologist Callum Roberts is 'en route to becoming one of humankind's most serious impacts on the sea'.[15] About one-third of the carbon dioxide released into the atmosphere is absorbed by seawater. This helps mitigate the effect of carbon emissions, but makes the sea more acidic. Although the increased acidity is very slight, and does not

Massive walrus haul-out near Point Lay, Alaska, 2010, possibly caused by decline in sea ice as a result of climate change.

harm mammals, it is very serious for other organisms such as molluscs, crustaceans and corals. These animals build their shells and skeletons from chalky carbonate dissolved in seawater. However, more acidic seawater contains less carbonate, making it more difficult for molluscs and crustaceans to grow shells and skeletons. With Arctic seas likely to be among the most severely affected by ocean acidification, the survival of the walrus's key prey species is in danger. Bottom-dwelling molluscs may also be adversely affected by the loss of sea ice. The underside of the ice is home to sea ice algae, which drifts down to provide food for animals on the sea floor. Less ice means less algae, which means less food for the molluscs. In warmer temperatures, there tends to be more zooplankton competing with bottom-dwelling animals for food. There are winners as well as losers in any environmental change and among the winners might be sub-Arctic fish, such as the walleye pollock, which feed on zooplankton and could find new habitats opening up in northerly waters that were previously too cold for them. These fish have the advantage of mobility. Unlike fish, molluscs cannot move in search of a more congenial habitat.

One animal that is definitely moving northwards as a result of the warmer climate is man. Climate change is opening up the potential for developing huge Arctic mineral deposits, including iron ore, copper, platinum, rare earth elements, uranium, gold and diamonds. Most significantly, the Arctic may contain as much as 25 per cent of the world's untapped oil and gas reserves, many of them located beneath the sea floor. These deposits are very attractive to nations eager to reduce dependence on imports from the unstable Middle East, and vast sums of money have been spent by the oil industry on exploratory drills and surveys. Shell alone has spent nearly $5 billion as of 2013. Hydrocarbon deposits have been found throughout the range of the walrus.

Development is proposed in the eastern Chukchi Sea among Pacific walrus feeding grounds and migration routes. Reserves have been discovered around Greenland, in the Laptev Sea and in the Barents, White and Kara Seas. There are eleven fields in the Barents Sea alone, including the Shtokman gas field, the largest in the world.

Concern about the development of these reserves has focused on the dangers of an oil spill. Although there have been no reported walrus oilings, walruses are thought to be more vulnerable to oil spills than other sea mammals. Their preferred habitats of coasts and pack ice are areas where oil is likely to accumulate, and their gregarious behaviour, means that large numbers of animals would be affected. Furthermore, the walrus's late age of sexual maturity and low birth rate would make it difficult to recover from a large population loss. Oil sinks and would kill prey species, and persists for decades. Over their long lives walruses could accumulate high levels of contaminants while digging on the sea floor. A WWF Russia report into the isolated Atlantic walrus population of the southeastern Barents Sea concluded that a large spill 'would inevitably entail irreversible consequences of the entire ecosystem, and the walrus group would not survive due to the collapse of forage resources and direct pollution of the animals with oil'.[16]

Arctic weather and ice conditions make drilling on the seabed, transportation of extracted oil and removal of any spilled material extremely problematic. After the *Exxon Valdez* oil spill in 1989 in Prince William Sound, Alaska, clean-up operations were hampered by the remote location and bad weather. Out of the 11 million gallons of oil spilled, only a small percentage was ever recovered. So far, safety issues have drilling attempts in northern waters. In December 2011 the *Kolskaya*, a Russian mobile drilling rig, capsized in a storm in the Sea of Okhotsk with the loss of 53 lives.[17] A year later a Shell rig, the *Kulluk*, ran aground in Alaska when rough seas prevented its attachment to a tug.[18] There have already been minor spills. In May 2011 beaches were oiled in Kandalaksha Bay on the White Sea.[19] Russia has a particularly poor safety record. Greenpeace estimate that over 5 million tonnes of oil is spilled there every year, seven times the amount leaked from the catastrophic *Deepwater Horizon* blow-out in the Gulf of Mexico in 2010.[20]

Despite its apparently pristine beauty, the Arctic is already highly polluted: not by local industries, but by those thousands of miles to the south. As a result of atmospheric and ocean currents, chemicals never used in the Arctic are swept northwards, accumulating in the sea and the bodies of its inhabitants. Substances known as POPs – persistent organic pollutants – are resistant to biodegradation. When they enter an animal's body they cannot be broken down, so they are stored in fat and pass up the food chain when the animal is eaten. As high-level predators, sea mammals accumulate large amounts of these toxins. Walruses feed fairly low on the food chain, and so few (probably seal-eaters) have been recorded with such high pollutant levels as seals, bears or whales.[21] However, if mollusc populations decline or lack of sea ice prevents walruses reaching feeding grounds, more walruses might turn to seals, and increase their pollutant levels. Among the most widespread POPs are organochlorides, a group of chemicals used in pesticides, coolants and solvents. These have been linked to hermaphrodism in polar bears and increased mortality in epidemics of seal distemper. Other possible health effects include hormonal changes, suppression of the immune system and impaired cognition. Many harmful chemicals, such as PCBs and DDT, the insecticide featured in Rachel Carson's environmental classic *Silent Spring* (1962), have been phased out, but new ones continue to be identified. PBDEs, widely used as flame retardants on electrical devices, have been found in many Arctic animals. No one knows what the long-term consequences of this contamination will be, for animals or people.[22]

All human activities in the Arctic have the potential to harm wildlife, and all human activities are increasing, risking more pollution and more disturbance. New fisheries may open up in the region, competing for walrus prey species, and damaging the sea-bed. In the 1980s the walrus colony on the Svalbard island of Moffen was besieged by illegal scallop fishermen in defiance of protection laws.[23] Such were the profits to be made that, indifferent to police and coastguards, the fishermen continued until the scallop population collapsed. Terrestrial mining projects, proposed near walrus habitats on Baffin Island and other areas, use dangerous chemicals and require increased shipping. Russia is actively developing the Northeast Passage, now usually known as the Northern Sea Route, which sees more shipping every year. Not all traffic is industrial: Arctic tourism is also on the rise. Even seemingly harmless walrus-watching ecotourists can cause dangerous disturbance if they approach too near. All ships create noise, and frequently leak oil and other pollutants. Less ice means ships can make a noise and leak oil in previously inaccessible locations. Noise is hazardous below water as well as above. Oil surveys make seismic blasts, and military craft use sonar. Both are disruptive to marine mammal communication, and can permanently impair animals' hearing.

Walruses may not be able to hear each other's songs.

Of course, walruses may adapt; they have survived much in the past. The higher temperatures will not be harmful in themselves: historically, walruses have lived in more southerly latitudes. Within the last 10,000–12,000 years there have been a number of climate change events causing loss of sea ice. The location of fossil walruses indicates that populations survived these periods by following the ice northwards, as in seasonal migration patterns. Perhaps as some habitats are lost, more northerly territory may open up. Walruses may escape old predators or gain new ones. New prey species might arrive as others decline. Warmer seas may bring new competitors or new diseases. Nobody knows. However, past adaptations occurred over long periods and today's climate change is much faster, and is coupled with additional stresses created by increased human presence in the Arctic. Walruses once thrived in the Gulf of St Lawrence, but would find it different now.

This concatenation of environmental circumstances has led to a marked increase in walrus orphans. In 2004 scientists on a u.s. Coast Guard vessel observed nine walrus calves swimming alone far out at sea, a previously unheard of phenomenon. Mother walruses usually leave their calves on sea ice while they feed, but without ice may have been forced to abandon them. The walrus calves approached the ship, but the crew were unable to help them. The biologist Carin Ashjian described the distressing scene: 'the poor little guys would just bark at us for hours on end. It was really awful. I wouldn't go outside'.[24] The incident resonated outside the scientific community (the romantic novelist Beth Orsoff was even inspired to write a love story set in a walrus sanctuary).[25] In July 2012 three abandoned baby walruses had better luck. Found by local residents of Barrow, Alaska, they were rescued by the Alaska Sealife Center. One died soon after, but the other two were successfully raised and rehomed in two u.s. zoos. YouTube videos of the walruses posted by the Center generated more than 150,000 Internet hits, prompting the journalist Julia O'Malley to comment 'videos of baby walruses cuddling with people and each other are why the Internet was invented'. O'Malley visited the walruses herself, and reported gratifyingly that 'snuggling with a baby walrus feels like being pinned under a warm, very chubby person who is wearing a damp velour jumpsuit that smells faintly, almost pleasantly, like low tide.'[26]

There is a long history of humans adopting walrus orphans. From the first recorded instance of a captive walrus calf, presented to James I of England in 1608, to the walrus companions of Jacques Cousteau and Lord Dufferin, a former Governor General of Canada, walrus calves seem, perhaps surprisingly, to make excellent pets (but don't try this at home). Even the hardened walrus hunter James Lamont was not immune to the charms of a young walrus called Tommy, who 'became a great pet with the men; a dear, loving little creature, combining the affection of a spaniel with the proportions of a prize pig'.[27] But dear, loving creatures though they might be, pet walruses have always been short-lived; with the exception, that is, of Señor.

According to the Canadian newspaper the *Daily British Colonist* in 1881, Señor was the walrus companion of thirteen years standing of the Spanish sailor Captain DeAbortiz, who found him in the Bering Strait and trained him to answer to the blast of a silver whistle. The newspaper gave a full account of Señor's intriguing habits:

He eats bread and meat, enjoys tea and tobacco. He is as passionately fond of beer as an old toper, and on many occasions has become genteely 'tight' from imbibing too heavily . . . As the Captain good-naturedly remarked, as he showed the brute to a few visitors, he is becoming 'one big noosance.' In bright weather he sleeps in the sun on deck. During heavy blows he resorts to a kennel, but when the weather is calm he leaps overboard and sports about the ship for hours, catching and eating fish. When tired of swimming he is hauled on board in a great iron basket. On one occasion, off the Cape of Good Hope, a great shark tackled Señor, laying hold of one of his paws and biting off two of his toes, but Señor dove, and coming up under his enemy's belly, ripped him up with one thrust of his great tusks, and devoured him with savage cries of delight and satisfaction. He is very fond of the Captain, and when the latter has been absent from the ship for a day or two he manifests his uneasiness by a thundering noise not unlike the sound that might be emitted by two or three scores of dogs barking in chorus.[28]

This story spread widely at the time, appearing in the *New York Times* and in the European press, stimulating great interest and a request to purchase the walrus from an American circus proprietor. But alas, this tea-drinking, smoking, shark-fighting, drunken 'noosance' of a walrus was nothing more than an April Fool perpetrated by the *Colonist*. The response to the story was so overwhelming that the *Colonist* was led to publish a confession two months later, asking of Señor's celebrity, 'When will it finally stop and the poor old walrus be allowed to "take a rest?"'[29]

Señor could never have been real. Looking after a walrus is a considerable challenge for humans. The first walrus acquired by

London Zoo died after only three days, 'probably from having been fed on a diet so unnatural to it as oatcake', according to Mr A. Newton of the Zoological Society.[30] The most successful keeper of walruses in captivity was German zoo entrepreneur Carl Hagenbeck, who pioneered the modern-style zoo in which animals are kept in enclosures resembling their natural habitats rather than in cages with bars. Walruses and seals featured in his first 'Eismeer Panorama', opened in the 1890s. As many as eight walruses at a time were kept alongside seals, reindeer, polar

P.Z.S. 1909 PL. LXXVI.

YOUNG WALRUS (ODOBÆNUS ROSMARUS).

An ill-fated baby walrus at London Zoo in 1908, one of two which died within a few weeks of arrival. From a watercolour by Carton Moore-Park, in P. Chalmers Mitchell, *Proceedings of the Zoological Society of London* (1909).

Carl Hagenbeck and a keeper feed the walruses, 1912.

bears and (the geographically inappropriate) penguins in an approximation of an Arctic scene. Hagenbeck must be one of the few people ever to have his portrait painted with a walrus. His zoo in Hamburg, run by his descendants, is one of the few European institutions to keep walruses today.

Nowadays advances in zoo practice and veterinary science allow walruses to lead long lives in zoos, but animal welfare organizations and some zoo professionals are uncomfortable with sea mammals in captivity, arguing that keeping migratory, herd animals in small numbers in a restricted environment is in itself cruel. And although in the u.s. captive walruses are always rescued orphans that would otherwise have died, this is not the case elsewhere. In 2012 Russian plans to capture 150 walrus calves for sale to zoos and oceanariums, which would involve killing 150 walrus mothers, caused concern among indigenous communities.[31] Even if they survive to adulthood, captive walruses can suffer a number of health problems, including skin and eye problems from chlorinated water, tusk damage and ingestion of foreign objects. As for many species, boredom is a serious problem for walruses. Bored walruses can manifest disturbing behaviour such as swimming in circles, food regurgitation and self-abuse. Zoo staff combat these problems by training programmes and habitat enhancement. One u.s. zoo has experimented with putting mats stuffed with fish and molluscs on to the bottoms of the walrus tanks so that the walruses can eat as they would in the wild.[32] The most familiar training programmes feature walruses performing 'tricks', such as dancing, doing exercise routines or playing musical instruments, for human entertainment. Such routines involve extensive human contact and attention, which may be preferable to solitary swimming around a tank.

The scientific and educational work of zoos may benefit walruses, not least by raising the profile of a potentially endangered species, but the survival of walruses in marine parks and

Hagenbeck's 'Eismeer Panorama', with walruses and penguins, c. 1911.

research facilities would be no survival for the species at all, but a desultory half life. If the walrus requires saving, it must be saved in its own environment. Perhaps ironically, if walrus numbers decline, walrus hunters are the humans with most to lose. Working alongside scientists, indigenous people are increasingly taking a leading role on environmental issues. Sheila Watt-Cloutier, the leader of the Inuit Circumpolar Council, was instrumental in the banning of harmful pollutants in the Stockholm Convention of 2004. Traditional ecological knowledge (TEK) has become a valued element in climate change research. In response to the recent huge walrus haul-outs in Chukotka and Alaska, local volunteers cleaned beaches and set up monitoring programmes to minimize disturbance. Chukchi hunters have returned to using spears when hunting near the haul-outs as gunfire can cause stampedes.[33] The village of Ryrkaypiy (or 'Place of Walrus' in Chukchi) has become well known for its proximity to the massive haul-outs. To draw attention to the issues, with the support of WWF Russia and the Marine Mammal Council (a Russian NGO), 'International Walrus Day' (24 November), has been celebrated in the village since 2008. In 2013 a new protected nature reserve was established in the area.

The threats facing the walrus cannot be addressed on a purely local level, however. So far, international efforts to agree a reduction of carbon emissions have been fraught with difficulty, a situation not helped by vigorous climate-change denial, often funded by the powerful energy lobby. Today's environmental (and walrus) exploitation mirrors that of the past. Historically, humans endangered walruses directly. They were useful commodities to be killed, boiled up and consumed by the fires of industry. This second human threat is an indirect one, but it is the same never-ending quest for energy and economic growth that drives climate change and, as one writer puts it, 'the global scramble for the world's last resources'.[34] No factory owner today would use

walrus-hide belting or light his lamps with blubber oil – it would be culturally unacceptable, and besides, much better synthetic substitutes are available – but industry still depends on unsustainable consumption of resources. Walruses are no longer useful to industry, but they, and their human supporters, get in its way.

In 2008 the environmental group the Center for Biological Diversity petitioned the u.s. government to list the Pacific walrus as an endangered species, on the grounds that 'unless we take drastic action to reduce greenhouse pollution, the grim reaper of global warming will ultimately claim the Pacific walrus as a victim'.[35] The u.s. Fish and Wildlife Service concluded that the listing was warranted, but that other species had higher priority. This decision must have come as a relief to some, since listing of the walrus under the u.s. Endangered Species Act would increase restrictions on Arctic developers. Concern for the Arctic ecosystem as a whole has sparked worldwide climate activism and opposition to development in the region. Greenpeace are

A baby walrus, Quebec Aquarium.

campaigning to create a global sanctuary around the North Pole, free from oil drilling and industrial fishing. Activists and industry are increasingly coming into conflict. In 2012 Shell unsuccessfully sued Greenpeace in an attempt to ban protests near its property. Arctic issues have attracted high-profile supporters such as Paul McCartney, who was moved to declare himself a walrus when joining the online 'Arctic Rising' campaign.[36] The walrus is not alone.

For all its history of monstrosity, people in Western industrial culture seem now to love walruses. Señor may be taken as an exemplum of our attraction to these singular creatures. New York's Mayor Bloomberg said that a rare walrus calf born in captivity in the city's aquarium had 'melted the hearts of millions'.[37] In *National Geographic*'s film *Arctic Tale* (2007), walruses take their place alongside polar bears as 'poster animals' for the climate change debate. The popular view of walruses has come a long way since a newspaper account of 1887 described the walrus as 'one of the most disgusting looking objects known to man'.[38] But, poised as we are on the threshold of global environmental disaster, attachment to the cute and the kitsch in how we represent and imagine walruses in the West only takes us so far. We need respect for walruses in their otherness from us; an ethical commitment that is not contingent on our amusement, advantage or profit. We still have the chance to mitigate the effects of climate change on the walrus, and of climate change itself. All our actions are haunted by the lives of other beings, by the distant, unintended effects of consumer culture. Global warming means that our lives and the lives of walruses come into a strange convergence. We are all the walrus.

Timeline of the Walrus

10–12 MYA	5–8 MYA	600,000 YA	28,000 YA
Archaic walruses emerge in the Pacific Ocean	The modern walrus appears in the Atlantic	Atlantic and Pacific walruses separate	First human habitation of the Arctic

1521	1534	1604	1608
Albrecht Dürer paints a walrus	Jacques Cartier finds walruses in North America	First walruses hunted on Spitsbergen	A baby walrus is presented to King James I

1872	1909–56	1951
Publication of 'The Walrus and the Carpenter' in *Through the Looking-Glass* by Lewis Carroll	Bans on non-indigenous walrus hunting in the U.S., Canada, Norway, Greenland and Russia	The walrus is Disneyfied in the film *Alice in Wonderland*

WALRUS TEETH!

WALRUS TEETH.   WALRUS TEETH.

THE HIGHEST MARKET PRICE PAID
for this article by   IRWIN & CO.
177-6m   Custom House Brokers, Rockhampton st.

AD 890	1456	1520
Viking adventurer Ohthere goes walrus hunting	A walrus found swimming up the Thames is eaten by Londoners	Bishop Valkendorf of Trondheim sends a salted walrus head to the Pope

1758	1800	1860
Scientific description of the walrus by Linnaeus	Extinction of Gulf of St Lawrence walrus herds	American whalers turn their attention to Bering Strait walrus herds

1967	2007	2008
The Beatles release 'I am the Walrus'	Thousands of walruses die in stampedes on Russian beaches	Center for Biological Diversity petitions the U.S. government for Pacific walrus to be listed as an endangered species as a result of climate change

References

1 THE WALRUS EMERGES

1 G. Carleton Ray, 'Walrus, the Beringian "Tooth-walker"', in *Gifts from the Ancestors: Ancient Ivories of Bering Strait*, ed. William W. Fitzhugh, Julia Hollowell and Aron L. Crowell (Princeton, NJ, 2009), p. 46.

2 So-called by Norwegian explorer Otto Sverdrup in *New Land: Four Years in the Arctic Regions*, trans. Ethel Harriet Hearn (London, 1904), vol. I, p. 185.

3 Elisha Kent Kane, *Arctic Explorations in Search of Sir John Franklin* (London, 1877), p. 246.

4 Froelich Rainey, quoted in Fred Bruemmer, *Seals in the Wild* (Toronto, 1998), p. 209.

5 William Caxton, quoted in Jay Alan Levenson, *Circa 1492: Art in the Age of Exploration* (New Haven, CT, 1991), p. 300.

6 Edmund Spenser, *The Faerie Queene* (London, 1596), Book II, Canto xii, verse 24.

7 Olaudah Equiano, *The Interesting Narrative of the Life of Olaudah Equiano, or Gustavus Vassa, the African Slave, written by Himself*, ed. Werner Sollors (New York, 2001), p. 132.

8 Sir Everard Home, *Lectures on Comparative Anatomy* (London, 1814), vol. I, pp. 249–50.

9 Sir Everard Home, 'Some Curious Facts Respecting the Walrus and Seal, Discovered by the Examination of Specimens Brought to England by the Different Ships Lately Returned from the Polar Circle', *Philosophical Transactions of the Royal Society of London*, CXIV (March, 1824).

10 The genus *Trichechus* now has the manatee as its only member, but has a legacy in the Italian name for the walrus, *tricheco*.

11 See C. Lindqvist et al., 'The Laptev Sea Walrus *Odobenus rosmarus laptevi*: An Enigma Revisited', *Zoologica Scripta*, XXXVIII (2009), pp. 113–27.

12 For a description of the evolution of the walrus, see Annalisa Berta, James L. Sumich and Kit M. Kovacs, *Marine Mammals: Evolutionary Biology* (London, 2006), pp. 27–47.

13 For an accessible scientific account of the Pacific walrus, see Francis H. Fay, 'Ecology and Biology of the Pacific Walrus, *Odobenus Rosmarus Divergens* Illiger', *North American Fauna*, LXXIV (1982).

14 The most recent population survey in 2006 found 129,000 Pacific walruses, but as some areas were unable to be reached it is likely that this is an underestimate of the true population.

15 Carlos Nores and Concepción Pérez, 'The Occurrence of Walrus (*Odobenus rosmarus*) in Southern Europe', *Journal of Zoology* (London), XXVVI (December, 1988), pp. 593–6.

16 Samuel Purchas, *Hakluytus Postumus, or Purchas His Pilgrimes* (Glasgow, 1906), vol. XIII, pp. 266–7.

17 Victor Scheffer, *A Natural History of Marine Mammals* (New York, 1976), p. 39.

18 Unlike many other seal species, it is their soft white baby fur, or lanugo, which has made baby harp seals a target for commercial hunters. In walruses the lanugo disappears in the womb.

19 Fay, 'Ecology and Biology', p. 46.

20 N. Levermann et al., 'Feeding Behaviour of Free-ranging Walruses with Notes on Apparent Dextrality of Flipper Use', *BMC Ecology*, III (2003), see www.biomedcentral.com.

21 R. A. Kastelein and M. A. Van Gaalen, 'The Sensitivity of the Vibrissae of a Pacific Walrus (*Odobenus rosmarus divergens)* Part 1, in *Aquatic Mammals*, XIV (1988).

22 Fay, 'Ecology and Biology', p. 71.

23 Peter Freuchen, 'Field Notes and Biological Observations', in *Report of the Fifth Thule Expedition 1921–24. Zoology I: Mammals* (Copenhagen, 1935), vol. II, No. 4–5, p. 244.

24 Ibid., p. 251.

25 Thomas Pennant, *Arctic Zoology* (London, 1784), vol. I, p. 147.

26 James Cook, quoted in Robert Kerr, *A General History and Collection of Voyages and Travels* (London, 1824), vol. XVI, p. 346.

27 See Ø. Wiig, I. Gjertz and D. Griffiths, 'Migration of Walruses (*Odobenus rosmarus*) in the Svalbard and Franz Josef Land Area', *Journal of Zoology*, CCXXXVIII (April, 1996).

28 Jacques-Yves Cousteau and Philippe Diolé, *Sea Lion, Elephant Seal, Walrus*, trans. J. F. Bernard (London, 1974), pp. 241–3.

29 Sir James Lamont, *Seasons with the Sea-horses* (New York, 1861), p. 82.

30 Ibid., p. 70.

31 Francis H. Fay, 'The Pacific Walrus (*Odobenus rosmarus divergens*): Spatial Ecology, Life History and Population', PhD dissertation, University of British Colombia (1955), p. 67.

32 Robert Southey, *The Life of Nelson* (London, 1814), vol. I, p. 15.

33 Purchas, *Hakluytus Postumus*, vol. XIII, p. 276.

34 See Matthew Brunwasser, 'Discovering Walruses', in *Living on Earth* (online, 2009), www.loe.org, accessed 20 January 2013.

35 'In and About the City', *New York Times*, 13 October 1884.

36 For more details of this research, see the website of the Pinniped Cognition and Sensory Systems Laboratory, University of California Santa Cruz: http://pinnipedlab.ucsc.edu.

2 WALRUSES AND THE INDIGENOUS ARCTIC

1 Knud Rasmussen and W. Worster, *Eskimo Folk Tales* (Copenhagen, 1921), p. 16.

2 Anthony Brandt, *The Man who Ate his Boots* (New York and Toronto, 2010), p. 382.

3 Robert McGhee, *Ancient People of the Arctic* (Vancouver, 1996), p. 136.

4 For more on the art of the Dorset culture, see Ingo Hessel, *Inuit Art: An Introduction* (London, 1998).

5 For detailed accounts of the early history of the Arctic, see John McCannon, *A History of the Arctic: Nature, Exploration and*

Exploitation (London, 2012) and Robert McGhee, *The Last Imaginary Place: A Human History of the Arctic World* (Chicago, IL, 2007).

6　'The Use of the Walrus', *London Reader*, 27 August 1881, p. 403.

7　Peter Freuchen, *Arctic Adventure* (New York, 1935), p. 83.

8　Frederick Schwatka, *Nimrod in the North* (New York, 1885), p. 46.

9　Freuchen, *Arctic Adventure*, p. 153.

10　Ibid., p. 191.

11　Irma S. Rombauer and Marion Rombauer Becker, *The Joy of Cooking* (New York, 1995), p. 819.

12　Henry W. Elliott, *Our Arctic Province: Alaska and the Seal Islands* (New York, 1886), pp. 455–6.

13　Charles Francis Hall, *Arctic Researches and Life amongst the Esquimaux* (New York, 1865), p. 522.

14　Zona Spray Starks, 'Arctic Foodways and Contemporary Cuisine', *Gastronomica*, 7 (2007), p. 48.

15　Schwatka, *Nimrod in the North*, pp. 35–6.

16　Ibid., p. 35.

17　Elisha Kent Kane, *Arctic Explorations in Search of Sir John Franklin* (London, 1877), pp. 274–5.

18　Richard Hough, *Captain James Cook: A Biography* (London, 1994), p. 395.

19　See James A. Fall and Molly B. Chythlook, 'The Round Island Walrus Hunt: Reviving a Cultural Tradition', Cultural Survival, XXII/3 (Fall 2008), at www.culturalsurvival.org.

20　Freuchen, *Arctic Adventure*, p. 154.

21　For a first-hand account of a traditional Inuit walrus hunt, see Jean Malaurie, *The Last Kings of Thule*, trans. Adrienne Foulke (Chicago, IL, 1982), pp. 62–71.

22　Hall, *Arctic Researches*, p. 500.

23　The walrus penis resides in an abdominal sheath extending along the animal's belly, possibly making it vulnerable to breakage when bumping over uneven ice.

24 Edward W. Nelson, *The Eskimo about Bering Strait* (Washington, DC, 1900), p. 166.

25 Fridtjof Nansen, *Eskimo Life*, trans. William Archer (New York, 1893), p. 75.

26 Boas, 'The Eskimo of Baffin and Hudson Bay', *Bulletin of the American Museum of Natural History* (New York), XV (1901), p. 116.

27 Knud Rasmussen, *The People of the Polar North: A Record*, trans. and ed. G. Herring (London, 1908), p. 143.

28 Boas, 'The Eskimo', p. 123.

29 Ibid., p. 123.

30 Frédéric B. Laugrand and Jarich G. Oosten, *Inuit Shamanism and Christianity: Transitions and Transformations in the Twentieth Century* (Montreal, 2010), p. 206.

31 John Moss, ed., *Echoing Silence: Essays on Arctic Narrative* (Ottawa, 1997), p. 230.

32 Knud Rasmussen, *Intellectual Culture of the Iglulik Eskimos* (Copenhagen, 1929), pp. 118–19.

33 Ibid., p. 113.

34 Henry Rink, *Tales and Traditions of the Eskimo* (Edinburgh, 1875), p. 59.

35 Stefan Donecker, 'The Lion, the Witch and the Walrus: Images of the Sorcerous North in the 16th and 17th Centuries', in *TRANS. Internet-Zeitschrift für Kulturwissenschaften*, 17 (2010).

36 See Walter J. Hoffman, *The Graphic Art of the Eskimos* (Washington, 1897).

37 Lars Krutak, 'Tattoos of the Early Hunter-gatherers of the Arctic' (2000), at www.larskrutak.com, accessed 21 January 2013.

38 Basil Dmytryshyn, E.A.P. Crownhart-Vaughan and Thomas Vaughan, ed. and trans., *Russia's Conquest of Siberia: A Documentary Record* (Oregon, 1985), p. 229.

39 Edward S. Curtis, *The North American Indian*, vol. XX: *The Alaskan Eskimo. The Nunivak. The Eskimo of Hooper Bay. The Eskimo of King Island. The Eskimo of Little Diomede Island. The Eskimo of Cape Prince of Wales. The Kotzebue Eskimo. The Noatak. The Kobuk. The Selawik* (Norwood, MA, 1930), p. 74.

40 Roger Silook, in William W. Fitzhugh, Julia Hollowell and Aron
   L. Crowell, eds, *Gifts from the Ancestors: Ancient Ivories of Bering
   Strait* (Princeton, NJ, 2009), p. 217.
41 Neil Christopher, Neil McDermott and Louise Flaherty, *Unikkaaqtuat:
   An Introduction to Traditional Inuit Myths and Legends* (Toronto,
   2011), p. 160.
42 Freuchen, *Arctic Adventure*, p. 137.

3 THE WAR ON THE WALRUS

 1 'Ohthere's Voyage', in *King Alfred's Anglo-Saxon Version of the
   Compendious History of the World by Orosius,* ed. and trans. Joseph
   Bosworth (London, 1859), pp. 41–2.
 2 The walrus is no longer found off the Norwegian coast, although
   it is possible that walruses were once found in number around
   Scandinavia but were hunted to extinction in these waters prior to
   Ohthere's time. The Norwegian explorer Fridtjof Nansen identified
   several place names along the Norwegian coast that indicate the
   past presence of walruses, such as Rosmålvik and Rosmålen. They
   are occasional visitors today.
 3 Albert the Great, *Man and the Beasts (De Animalibus, books 22–26)*,
   trans. James J. Scanlan (Binghampton, NY, 1987), p. 341.
 4 See 'Maeshow's Runes: Viking Graffiti', www.orkneyjar.com,
   accessed 19 June 2013.
 5 Scanlan, *Albert the Great*, pp. 340–41.
 6 Poul Nørlund, quoted in Kirsten A. Seaver, *The Frozen Echo:
   Greenland and the Exploration of North America, c. AD 1000–1500*
   (Stanford, CA, 1996), p. 31.
 7 For the story of the Bury Cross, see Denis Blomfield-Smith,
   The Walrus Said: A Long Silence is Broken (Sussex, 2004).
 8 See Chris Lavers, *The Natural History of Unicorns* (London,
   2009).
 9 Richard Hakluyt, *The Principal Navigations, Voyages, Traffiques
   and Discoveries of the English Nation* (Glasgow, 1904), vol. VIII,
   p. 157.

10 Hildegard of Bingen, *Causae et Curae,* quoted in Lynn Thorndike, *A History of Magic and Experimental Science* (New York, 1923), vol. II, p. 144.

11 Simon Wilkin, ed., *The Works of Sir Thomas Browne* (London, 1890), vol. I, p. 341.

12 Hakluyt, *Navigations*, vol. VIII, p. 70.

13 Ibid., pp. 192–3.

14 Ibid., p. 156.

15 Samuel Purchas, *Hakluytus Postumus, or Purchas his Pilgrimes* (Glasgow, 1906), vol. XIII, p. 268.

16 Robert Fotherby, 'Narrative of a Voyage to Spitzbergen in the Year 1613', ed. Samuel F. Haven, in *Transactions of the American Antiquarian Society*, IV (1860), pp. 313–14.

17 A. Howard Clark, 'The Pacific Walrus Fishery', in George Brown Goode, *The Fisheries and Fishery Industries of the United States, Section II* (Washington, DC, 1887), vol. V, p. 314.

18 John Bockstoce, *Whales, Ice and Men: The History of Whaling in the Western Arctic* (Seattle, WA, 1986), p. 130.

19 Ibid., p. 138.

20 Waldemar Bogoras, 'The Chukchee', Part III: *Memoir of the American Museum of Natural History (The Jesup North Pacific Expedition)* (New York, 1904), vol. XI, p. 731. The Ker'ek did not recover from the decimation of the walrus herds. The Russian census of 2010 records only four individuals remaining.

21 'Goods Entered into Customhouse Yesterday', *Courier and Argus* (Dundee, Scotland), 14 November 1900.

22 John J. Underwood, *Alaska: An Empire in the Making* (New York, 1913), p. 71.

23 Lord Tweedsmuir, *Hudson's Bay Trader* (London, 1951), p. 14.

24 Duc de Orléans, *Hunters and Hunting in the Arctic* (London, 1911), p. 128.

25 Agnes Herbert, *Two Dianas in Alaska* (London and New York, 1909).

26 Sir James Lamont, *Seasons with the Sea-horses* (London, 1861), p. 5.

27 Sir James Lamont, *Yachting in the Arctic Seas* (London, 1876), p. 192.

28 Lamont, *Seasons*, p. 66.
29 'The White Sea Fisheries', *The Times* (London), 11 March 1911.
30 Sir Harry Johnston, *British Mammals* (London, 1903), pp. 194–5.
31 'Walrus Swarm Machine-gunned', *Tri City Herald* (Washington State), 16 March 1959.

4 WALRUSES IN POPULAR AND VISUAL CULTURE

1 Fridtjof Nansen, *Farthest North* (London, 1897), vol. II, p. 339.
2 Peter Davidson, *The Idea of North* (London, 2005), pp. 33–4.
3 Quoted in Gwyn Jones, *A History of the Vikings* (Oxford, 1968), p. 195.
4 Trans. Andy Orchard, in *Pride and Prodigies: Studies in the Monsters of the Beowulf Manuscript* (Toronto, 2003), p. 289.
5 Carl Phelpstead, ed., *A History of Norway and the Passion and Miracles of the Blessed Óláfr*, trans. Devra Kunin (London, 2001), p. 4.
6 *The King's Mirror (Konungs skuggsjá)*, trans. Laurence Marcellus Larson (New York, 1917), p. 135; p. 122.
7 See John J. McKay, 'Mammoth Tales', at http://mammothtales. blogspot.co.uk, for an intriguing discussion of the Strasbourg walrus and other sea monsters.
8 Brian W. Ogilvie, *The Science of Describing: Natural History in Renaissance Europe* (Chicago, IL, 2006), p. 233.
9 Quoted in John J. Mckay, 'The White Elephant of Rucheni', *Scientific American*, 11 November 2011.
10 Ibid.
11 At www.britishmuseum.org, accessed 23 January 2013.
12 N. Krag and S. Stephanius, quoted in Charles G. M. Paxton and R. Holland, 'Was Steenstrup Right? A New Interpretation of the 16th Century Sea Monk of the Øresund', *Steenstrupia*, XXIX/1 (2005), p. 39.
13 William Scoresby, *An Account of the Arctic Regions, with a History and Description of the Northern Whale-Fishery* (Edinburgh, 1820), vol. I, p. 504.

14 A. E. Nordenskiöld, *The Voyage of the Vega round Asia and Europe*, trans. Alexander Leslie (New York, 1882), vol. I, pp. 263–4.

15 Ogilvie, *Natural History*, p. 235.

16 Georges-Louis Leclerc, Comte de Buffon, *Buffon's Natural History, Containing a Theory of the Earth, a General History of Man etc.*, trans. Anonymous (London, 1807), vol. IX, p. 85.

17 Ibid., p. 85.

18 Charles F. Hall, *Narrative of the Second Expedition of Charles F. Hall*, ed. J. E. Nourse (Washington, DC, 1879), p. 120.

19 Mary Shelley, *Frankenstein* (Oxford, 1993), p. 176.

20 See Stephen Knight, 'The Arctic Arthur', *Arthuriana*, XXI/2 (2011), pp. 59–89.

21 R. M. Ballantyne, *Ungava: A Tale of Esquimau Land* (London, 1917), pp. 316–18.

22 R. M. Ballantyne, *The Walrus Hunters* (London, 1910), p. 260; p. 373.

23 Edward Lear, 'Cold are the Crabs that Crawl on Yonder Hill', in *The Complete Nonsense and Other Verse* (London, 2002), p. 386.

24 Lewis Carroll, *Alice's Adventures in Wonderland and Through the Looking-Glass*, ed. Hugh Haughton (Oxford, 1982), pp. 162–6.

25 As reported by BBC North East, 'Coast: Point Wear: The Carroll Connection', www.bbc.co.uk, accessed 21 January 2013.

26 Hugh Haughton, ed., explanatory notes to Carroll *Alice's Adventures in Wonderland*, p. 340.

27 Ibid.

28 Quoted in George P. Landow, 'Charles Dodgson and Contemporary Politics', www.victorianweb.org, accessed 21 January 2013.

29 J. B. Priestley, 'The Walrus and the Carpenter', *New Statesman*, 10 August 1957, p. 168.

30 Henry Kingsley, *Valentin: A French Boy's Story of Sedan* (London, 1872), vol. I, p. 152.

31 Michael E. Roos, 'The Walrus and the Deacon: John Lennon's Debt to Lewis Carroll', *Journal of Popular Culture*, XVIII/10 (1984), p. 26.

32 Ibid., p. 26; p. 27.

33 Meredith Bennett-Smith, 'One Million Moms Decries Bestiality Themes in New Walrus Skittles Ad', *Huffington Post*, www.huffingtonpost.com, accessed 21 January 2013.

34 Laurie Foos, *Portrait of the Walrus by a Young Artist* (London, 1998).

35 Jane Austen and Ben H. Winters, *Sense and Sensibility and Sea Monsters* (Philadelphia, PA, 2009).

5 WALRUSES IN A WARMING WORLD

1 J. Bernard Gilpin, 'On the Walrus', *Proceedings and Transactions of the Nova Scotian Institute of Science*, II/3 (1869), p. 127.

2 Alaska History and Cultural Studies Website, www.akhistorycourse.org, accessed 21 January 2013.

3 Ibid.

4 See James A. Fall and Molly B. Chythlook, 'The Round Island Walrus Hunt: Reviving a Cultural Tradition', *Cultural Survival Quarterly*, XXII/3 (1998), see www.culturalsurvival.org.

5 John Bennett and Susan Rowley, eds, *Uqalurait: An Oral History of Nunavut* (Montreal, 2004), p. 186.

6 See Laurel A. Neme, *Animal Investigators: How the World's First Wildlife Forensic Lab Is Solving Crimes and Saving Species* (New York, 2009), pp. 1–67.

7 C. J. Chivers, 'A Big Game', *New York Times*, 25 August 2002.

8 Michael Sandel, *What Money Can't Buy: The Moral Limits of Markets* (London, 2012), p. 84.

9 Joseph F. Bernard, 'Walrus Protection in Alaska', *Journal of Mammalogy*, VI/2 (May 1925), pp. 100–102.

10 Lars Witting and Erik W. Born, 'An Assessment of Greenland Walrus Populations', in *ICES Journal of Marine Science*, 62 (online, 2005); *Marine Mammal Commission Annual Report to Congress 2009* (Bethesda, MD, 2010), p. 65.

11 Igor Krupnik and G. Carleton Ray, 'Pacific Walruses, Indigenous Hunters, and Climate Change: Bridging Scientific and Indigenous Knowledge', *Deep Sea Research*, II/54 (2007), p. 2955.

12 John Vidal and Adam Vaughan, 'Artic sea ice shrinks to the smallest extent ever recorded', *The Guardian,* 14 September 2012.

13 For a thorough examination of threats to the Pacific walrus, see Joel Garlich-Miller et al., eds, *Status Review of the Pacific Walrus (Odobenus rosmarus divergens)* (Alaska, 2011).

14 Sea ice shrank to an even greater extent in 2012, with estimates of 100,000 walruses hauled out in Chukotka. Mortalities have not yet been reported.

15 Callum Roberts, *Ocean of Life: How Our Seas are Changing* (London, 2012), p. 97.

16 A. N. Boltunov, S. E. Belikov, Yu.A. Gorbunov, D. T. Menis and V. S. Semenova, *The Atlantic Walrus of the Southeastern Barents Sea and Adjacent Regions: Review of the Present Day Status* (Moscow, 2010), p. 25.

17 'Russia oil rig capsizes off Sakhalin, dozens missing', BBC News, 18 December 2011, www.bbc.co.uk.

18 *Alaska Dispatch,* 3 January 2013, see www.alaskadispatch.com.

19 *WWF Russian Arctic Bulletin* (April–May 2011), available online at www.wwf.ru.

20 'Black Ice: Russian Oil Disaster', www.greenpeace.org, accessed 19 June 2013.

21 E. W. Born, I. Gjertz and R. R. Reeves, 'Population Assessment of the Atlantic Walrus', *Meddelelser 138* (Oslo, 1995), p. 78.

22 For the full story of Arctic pollution, see Marla Cone, *Silent Snow: the Slow Poisoning of the Arctic* (New York, 2005).

23 Born et al., 'Population Assessment of the Atlantic Walrus', p. 80.

24 Carin Ashjian, quoted in 'Abandoned Walrus Calves Reported in the Arctic', in *Oceanus* online, www.whoi.edu, 2006.

25 Beth Orsoff, *How I Learned to Love the Walrus* (e-book, 2010), now reissued as *Girl in the Wild* (e-book, 2012).

26 Julia O'Malley, 'Alaska's Increasingly Famous Baby Walruses Just Want a Hug' in *Anchorage Daily News* online, 9 October 2012.

27 Sir James Lamont, *Yachting in the Arctic Seas* (London, 1876), p. 62.

28 'A Marine Monster', *Daily British Colonist* (Victoria, British Colombia), 1 April 1881.

29 'The Tame Walrus', *Daily British Colonist* (Victoria, British Colombia), 2 June 1881.

30 Alfred Newton, 'Notes on the Zoology of Spitzbergen', *Proceedings of the Zoological Society of London* (1864), p. 499.

31 'Joint Meeting on Pacific Walrus in Anchorage', *Haulout Keepers* online (December 2012), http://pacificwalrus.ru.

32 'The Effects of Foraging Mats as Enrichment in Captive Walruses (*Odobenus rosmarus*)', www.indiana.edu, accessed 13 January 2013.

33 Joel Garlich-Miller, 'Adapting to Climate Change: A Community Workshop on the Conservation and Management of Walruses on the Chukchi Sea Coast' (Barrow, AK, 2012), p.3. Paper published online at www.fws.org.

34 Michael T. Klare, *The Race for What's Left: The Global Scramble for the World's Last Resources* (New York, 2012)

35 Rebecca Noblin, Center for Biological Diversity Press Release (18 May 2009), www.biologicaldiversity.org.

36 Paul McCartney, 'Come Together, to Save the Arctic', *Huffington Post* (23 July 2012).

37 'Mourning a Beloved Walrus', *New York Times* (2 September 2009)

38 'The Walrus at Home', *Hampshire Telegraph and Sussex Chronicle etc.* (18 June 1887).

Select Bibliography

Allen, J. A., *History of North American Pinnipeds: A Monograph of the Walruses, Sea-lions, Sea-bears and Seals of North America* (Washington, 1880)

Ballantyne, R. M., *The Walrus Hunters* (London, 1910)

——, *Ungava: A Tale of Esquimau Land* (London, 1917)

Boas, Franz, 'The Eskimo of Baffin and Hudson Bay', *Bulletin of the American Museum of Natural History* (New York, 1901)

Bockstoce, John, *Whales, Ice and Men: The History of Whaling in the Western Arctic* (Seattle, WA, 1986)

Born, E. W., I. Gjertz and R. R. Reeves, 'Population Assessment of the Atlantic Walrus', *Meddelelser 138* (Oslo, 1995)

Bruemmer, Fred, *Seals in the Wild* (Toronto, 1998)

Carroll, Lewis, *Alice's Adventures in Wonderland and Through the Looking-Glass*, ed. Hugh Haughton (Oxford, 1982)

Christopher, Neil, *Kappianaqtut: Strange Creatures and Fantastic Beings from Inuit Myths and Legends* (Iqaluit, 2011)

Cone, Marla, *Silent Snow: The Slow Poisoning of the Arctic* (New York, 2005)

Cousteau, Jacques-Yves, and Philippe Diolé, *Sea Lion, Elephant Seal, Walrus,* trans. J. F. Bernard (London, 1974)

Elliott, Henry W., *Our Arctic Province: Alaska and the Seal Islands* (New York, 1886)

Fay, Francis H., 'Ecology and Biology of the Pacific Walrus, *Odobenus Rosmarus Divergens* Illiger', *North American Fauna*, LXXIV (Washington, 1982)

Freuchen, Peter, *Arctic Adventure* (New York, 1935)

Garlich-Miller, Joel, et al., eds, *Status Review of the Pacific Walrus (Odobenus rosmarus divergens)* (Alaska, 2011)

Hakluyt, Richard, *The Principal Navigations, Voyages, Traffiques and Discoveries of the English Nation* (Glasgow, 1904), vol. VIII

Hall, Charles Francis, *Arctic Researches and Life amongst the Esquimaux* (New York, 1865)

Hessel, Ingo, *Inuit Art: An Introduction* (London, 1998)

Kane, Elisha Kent, *Arctic Explorations in Search of Sir John Franklin* (London, 1877)

King, Judith E., *Seals of the World* (Oxford, 1983)

Knudtson, Peter, *The World of the Walrus* (San Francisco, CA, 1998)

Lamont, Sir James, *Seasons with the Sea-horses* (New York, 1861)

——, *Yachting in the Arctic Seas* (London, 1876)

Lavers, Chris, *The Natural History of Unicorns* (London, 2009)

McCannon, John, *A History of the Arctic: Nature, Exploration and Exploitation* (London, 2012)

McGhee, Robert, *Ancient People of the Arctic* (Vancouver, 1996)

——, *The Last Imaginary Place: A Human History of the Arctic World* (Chicago, IL, 2007)

McKay, John J., 'The White Elephant of Rucheni', *Scientific American* (guest blog, 2011)

Malaurie, Jean, *The Last Kings of Thule*, trans. Adrienne Foulke (Chicago, IL, 1985)

Mowat, Farley, *Sea of Slaughter* (Toronto, 1984)

Nansen, Fridtjof, *Farthest North*, 2 vols (London, 1897)

Ogilvie, Brian W., *The Science of Describing: Natural History in Renaissance Europe* (Chicago, IL, 2006)

Perry, Richard, *The World of the Walrus* (London, 1967)

Purchas, Samuel, *Hakluytus Postumus, or Purchas his Pilgrimes* (Glasgow, 1906), vol. XIII

Rasmussen, Knud, *The People of the Polar North: A Record*, trans. and ed. G. Herring (London, 1908)

Ray, Dorothy Jean, *A Legacy of Arctic Art* (Seattle, WA, 1996)

Riedman, Marianne, *The Pinnipeds: Seals, Sea Lions and Walruses* (Oxford, 1990)

Rink, Henry, *Tales and Traditions of the Eskimo: With a Sketch of their Habits, Religion, Language and Other Peculiarities* (Edinburgh, 1875)

Vaughan, Richard, *The Arctic: A History* (Stroud, 2007)

Associations and Websites

CONSERVATION ORGANIZATIONS

There is no one organization solely dedicated to worldwide walrus conservation.

ALASKA SEALIFE CENTER
An aquarium and research facility with a wildlife rescue programme
www.alaskasealife.org

WILDLIFE CONSERVATION SOCIETY
A U.S. conservation group based around New York's zoos
www.wcs.org

WORLD WILDLIFE FUND
There are various national websites. WWF Russia has a good English section with interesting walrus resources
www.wwf.ru

CAMPAIGNING ORGANIZATIONS

CENTER FOR BIOLOGICAL DIVERSITY
A U.S. group campaigning for the Pacific walrus to be listed as an endangered species
www.biologicaldiversity.org

Of particular relevance to walruses are the Save the Arctic campaign, and the Arctic Rising online movement
www.savethearctic.org
http://rising.savethearctic.org

SCIENTIFIC AND GOVERNMENTAL BODIES

ESKIMO WALRUS COMMISSION
The website of the organization representing the interests of indigenous walrus hunters in Alaska
www.kawerak.org

FISHERIES AND OCEANS CANADA
Information on the population and distribution of Canadian Atlantic walruses
www.dfo-mpo.gc.ca

GREENLAND INSTITUTE OF NATURAL RESOURCES
The walrus in Greenland
www.natur.gl

HAULOUT KEEPERS
The website of the project 'Guardians of the Walrus Haulouts' in Russian and English about the walrus monitoring project in Chukotka
http://pacificwalrus.ru

THE NORWEGIAN POLAR INSTITUTE
Information on the walrus populations of the Svalbard and Franz Josef Land archipelagos
www.npolar.no

U.S. FISH AND WILDLIFE SERVICE: MARINE MAMMAL MANAGEMENT
Information on the management of walrus populations
http://alaska.fws.gov

U.S. GEOLOGICAL SURVEY
Information on walrus tracking and the Pacific Walrus International
Database
http://alaska.usgs.gov

Acknowledgements

This book was conceived between northern Canada and the Kent coast. Sincere thanks are due to the University of Northern British Columbia for providing the funding to bring this project to life; thanks particularly to Kevin Hutchings for advice and encouragement, to Jessica Carey and Mackenzie Bowles for keeping cabin fever at bay in Prince George, and to Mary and the inter-library loans team at the Geoffrey A. Weller Library for being so helpful and always having a kind word. Thanks also to staff at the ZSL library, to Jonathan Burt for diligent and perceptive comments on the first draft and to Ruth Hawthorn for careful proof-reading and for entering the world of the walrus. Thanks lastly to Lily and Sophie for getting involved with the paperwork, and to Ginny Miller for joining in with the herd.

Photo Acknowledgements

The author and publishers wish to express their thanks to the below sources of illustrative material and / or permission to reproduce it:

Photo Architect of the Capitol, artist EverGreene Painting Studios: p. 97; copyright Estate of Kenojuak Ashevak, reproduced with permission of Dorset Fine Arts: p. 62; image courtesy of BoolaBoola2 at English Wikipedia: p. 99; photo Boston Public Library (archive.org) via Biodiversity Heritage Library: p. 166; courtesy British Museum, London (© The Trustees of the British Museum): pp. 12, 56, 60, 63, 74, 79, 91, 107, 118; image courtesy of Dave Cheadle of Dave's Great Cards eBay store: p. 137; photo courtesy Claumoho: p. 145; photo courtesy Eliezg: p. 156; image courtesy of Emmitsburg Historical Society: p. 119; image courtesy of Ginny from etsy.com: p. 40; reproduced courtesy of Stanton F. Fink via deviantART: p. 21; photo courtesy of Angelika C. J. Friebe Ltd, Dorking, Surrey: pp. 127, 153; photo courtesy Marc A. Garrett: p. 68; photo courtesy Glenbow Archives (NC-1-313): p. 163; photo copyright Horniman Museum and Gardens, London: p. 26; photo courtesy Oliver Kellhammer: p. 30; photo courtesy Kokstein: p. 123; courtesy Library of Congress, Prints & Photographs Division: pp. 10 (photo Lomen Bros. LC-DIG-ppmsc-01837), 46 (Edward S. Curtis Collection, LC-USZ62-107323), 48 (Edward S. Curtis Collection, LC-USZ62-46887), 49 (LC-DIG-ppmsc-01642), 51 (LC-DIG-ppmsc-02400), 66 (Edward S. Curtis Collection, LC-USZ62-13913), 100 (Edward S. Curtis Collection, LC-USZ62-74131), 144 (LC-DIG-cwpbh-03163, LC-DIG-ggbain-17575, LC-DIG-ggbain-20405, LC-DIG-cwpbh-05146, LC-DIG-cwpbh-03726,

Index

advertising, walruses in 136–40
Alaska Purchase 95–6, 97
Alaska Sealife Center 37, 162
Alcuin 112
Alfred, King of Wessex 14, 73
Arctic
    art 44–5, 62, 67–9, 98, 148,
    151–2
    as diabolic 111–12, 122
    conservation 169–70
    exploration 55–6, 84
    famine in 93
    indigenous peoples 8–11,
    42–5, 70
    maps of 113–16
    pollution 160–61, 168
    resource extraction 11,
    158–60
Arctic Small Tool tradition 43–4
Ashevak, Kenojuak 62, 151
Ashjian, Carin 162
Austen, Jane 141

Ballantyne, R. M. 124–7, 126
Barentsz, Willem 88, 89, 121

Beatles, The 134–5, 141
Boas, Franz 60, 62–3
Boece, Hector 76–7
Bible, the 107, 112
blubber 8, 10, 26, 31, 47, 50–51,
    55, 76, 86, 89–90, 94, 147
Bockstoce, John 92
Bogoras, Waldemar 93
Browne, Sir Thomas 83
Buchan, John 100
Buffon, Georges-Louis Leclerc,
    Comte de 121–2
Burghley, Lord 87
Bury Cross 81–2
butchering, of walruses 60–61

captivity, walruses in 17, 27, 29,
    35, 39, 41, 145, 162–8, 171
Carroll, Lewis 127–34, 136–7
Carson, Rachel (*Silent Spring*)
    160
Cartier, Jacques 86
cartoons, of walruses 79, 111, 128,
    132, 140–42, 145–6
Caxton, William 15

Chivers, C. J. 153–4
Chukchi 12–13, 47, 50, 70, 156, 168
climate change 11, 108, 155–8,
    162, 168, 171
Columbus, Christopher 83
communication, walrus 34–5
Cook, Captain James 19, 36, 55–6
Cousteau, Jacques 37, 163
Curtis, Edward S. 48, 66, 100

diet, of walruses 28–31
Disney, Walt (*Alice in
    Wonderland*) 140–41
Dorset culture 44–5
Doyle, Sir Arthur Conan 143, *144*
Dürer, Albrecht 116–17, *118*
Dusignathus 21

eating walrus 49–56, 78
Elliott, Henry W. 52–4, *61*, *78*
English Muscovy Company 87
elephants 18, 25, 75, 86, 97, 103,
    115–16
Elizabeth I, Queen of England 87
Equiano, Olaudah 16
Eskimo Walrus Commission 150,
    153
etymology 13–16
evolution, of walruses 20–22

Fay, Francis H. 29, 106
Foos, Laurie 141
Fotherby, Robert 88–90, *94*
Foyn, Svend 103
Franklin, Sir John 55, 122, *123*

Freuchen, Peter 30–31, 47, 50–51,
    58, 72
Fries, Laurent 115, *117*
Frobisher, Martin 43

Gessner, Conrad 14, 114–15
Gilbert, Sir Humphrey 84–5
Gilpin, J. Bernard 147–8
global warming *see* climate
    change
Greenpeace 169–71

Hagenbeck, Carl 165–6, *167*
Hall, Charles Francis 53–4, 59,
    122
Harryhausen, Ray 141, *142*
haul-outs 8, 31
Herbert, Agnes 101, *102*
hide, walrus 9–10, 26–7, 46,
    48–9, 61, 73, 75–6, 87, 94–5,
    96, 105, 169
Hildegard of Bingen, St 83
Historiae Animalium 15
Home, Sir Everard 18
Horniman Museum 26
Houston, James 151
Hughes, Merv 143
hunting, of walruses
    commercial 8–10, 22, 85–98,
    103–4, 106–8, 148
    indigenous 8–9, 11, 57–60,
    106, 148–50, 154–5
    sport 37–8, 98–103, 105,
    153–4
    Viking 75–7

Industrial Revolution 10, 94
intelligence, of walruses 39–41
Inuit 11, 40, 44–5, 49, 56–7
Inuktitut 13, 42–3, 48
Inupiat 45, 50–51, 155
ivory *see* tusks

James I, King of England 39, 163
James, Captain Thomas 87

Kane, Elisha Kent 9, 55
Katexac, Bernard Tuglamena
    152
Kennedy, President John F. 97
khutu 82–3
Kingsley, Henry 132
King's Mirror, The 112–13

Lamont, Sir James 37–8, 101–3,
    153, 163
Laptev Sea walruses 19, 22
Lear, Edward 127–8
Lennon, John 7, 133–5
Leo x, Pope 114–15
Lewis Chessmen 79
Liber monstrorum 112
Liddell, Alice 130
Linnaeus, Carl 17
London Zoo 164–5
Low, David 142–3
Lytton, Edward Bulwer
    (*King Arthur*) 122

McCartney, Paul 134–5, 171
McKay, John J. 115

Macmillan, Harold 132–3
Magnus, Albertus 75–6
Magnus, Olaus 77, 113
manatees 16–19
maternal care, by walruses 36–7,
    39
mermaids 12, 117–18
migration, of walruses 22–3
Milton, John (*Paradise Lost*)
    111–12
moustache 142–4 *see also*
    vibrissae

Nansen, Fridtjof 59–60, 109–11,
    122
Nelson, Horatio, Lord *34*, 38
Newell, Peter 128, *129*
Nietzsche, Friedrich 143, *144*
Nordenskiöld , Baron Nils Adolf
    Erik 119–20
Nørlund, Poul 78
Norse *see* Vikings
Northeast Passage 84, 88, 161
Northwest Passage 55, 84, 122
Nurivik see Sedna
Nunivak 48, 66, 70, 100

Odobenus 16–19
Ohthere 14, 73–5
oil, marine mammal 10, 50, 54,
    61, 73, 86, 92, 94, 169
Old Bering sea culture 44
O'Malley, Julia 162
One Million Moms 139–40
Orléans, Duke of 101

Orsoff, Beth 162
Ortelius, Abraham 113–14
Owen, Wilfred 142

Palaeo-Arctic 43–4, 69
Peake, Mervyn 128
Peary, Robert 56–7, *144*
Pennant, Thomas 34
pinnipeds *see* seals
poaching 104, 152–3, *154*
polar bears *33*, 35, 156
Poole, Jonas 23–4
population, of walruses 22–3,
     106, 147, 154–5
Priestley, J. B. 132
protection, of walruses 10,
     104–8, 148–9, 168–9

range, of walruses
     current 22–3, 85, 106
     historical 9–10, 76, 85–7, 96,
        106, 161
Rasmussen, Knud 42, 65
Rink, Henry 66
Roberts, Callum 157
Rombauer, Irma S. 51–2
Roos, Michael E. 134–5

Sami 14
Sandel, Michael 154
Savoonga 13, 45
Schwatka, Frederick 50, 54–5
Scoresby, William 118
scurvy, walrus meat as cure for
     55–6

seals
     hunting of 59, 84, 86, 88, 92,
        94–6, 104, 108
     in indigenous culture 12, 44,
        47–8, 50, 53–4, 58–9, 62–3,
        72, 118
     relationship to walrus 17, *18*,
        19, 24–5, 28–30, 35–6, 40,
        119, 160, 165
     species of 16–17, 20, 24, 28,
        35–6, 40, 95–6
sea monsters 8, 15–16, 84,
     108–13, 117–22, 141
Sedna 11–12, 62, 64–5
Seeganna Peter J. 152
Señor, a walrus 163–4, 171
sex 35–6, 40
shamanism 9, 44, 61–7, 69–72, 78
Shelley, Mary (*Frankenstein*) 122
Simpsons, The 7, 141, 143 4
singing, by walruses 35–6,
     40–41, 161
Six Flags Discovery Kingdom
     39–40
size, of walruses 24–5
sleeping, by walruses 33
Southey, Robert 38–9
Spenser, Edmund (*The Faerie
     Queen*) 15–16
Stadler, Craig 143
Stadukhin, Mikhail 70
Stalin 106, 132
Starks, Zona Spray 53–4
Steadman, Ralph 132
stench, of walruses 23, 35, 84

Stevenson, Robert Louis
(*Treasure Island*) 125–6
Sumner, Senator Charles 96

taboos 61–3
Talirunili, Joe 151
tattoos 68–9
Teevee, Ningeokuluk *152*
Tenniel, Sir John 128, 130, 136
Thule culture 44, 78
Tolkein, J.R.R. 13–14
trampolining 49, *51*
Trichechus see Odobenus
Tuniit *see* Dorset culture
tusks
    as commodity 8–10, 19, 73,
    75, 82, 93–5, 115
    as unicorn horn 82–3, 98, 117
    illegal taking of 152–3, *154*
    scrimshaw 10, 97–8, *99*
    medicinal value 83
    representation in art 113–15,
    117, 121–2, 124, 130, 135
    use by indigenous peoples
    10, 44–5, 47, 58, *60*, *63*,
    67–70, 97–8, *100*, 148–9, 152
    use by Vikings 14, *74*, 75–9
    use in medieval art 73, 79–83,
    87–8
    use in modern times 97–8,
    101, 105, 148
    use to walrus 20–21, 27–8, 31,
    32, 54, 64, 76, 164
Tweedsmuir, Lord 100

u.s. Fish and Wildlife Service
    150, 152, 154, 169
umiaq 48–9

Valkendorf, Bishop Erik 114–15
vibrissae *28*, 29, 35, 47, 124
Vikings 9, 14–15, 66–7, 73–9, 112,
    122

Waldeseemüller, Martin 115–16,
    117
Watt-Cloutier, Sheila 168
Wells, H. G. 143
whaling 87, 90–92, 93–4, 103,
    107, 155
White, Barry 143
Wilson, Harold 133

Yup'ik 13, 45, 49, 58, 93, 150